Local Livelihoods and Protected Area Management
Biodiversity Conservation Problems in Cameroon

Emmanuel Neba Ndenecho

Langaa Research & Publishing CIG
Mankon, Bamenda

Publisher:
Langaa RPCIG
Langaa Research & Publishing Common Initiative Group
P.O. Box 902 Mankon
Bamenda
North West Region
Cameroon
Langaagrp@gmail.com
www.langaa-rpcig.net

Distributed in and outside N. America by African Books Collective
orders@africanbookscollective.com
www.africanbookcollective.com

ISBN: 9956-717-54-1

© Ndenacho Emmanuel Neba 2011

DISCLAIMER
All views expressed in this publication are those of the author and do not necessarily
reflect the views of Langaa RPCIG.

Dedicated to Elizabeth; with the hope that her generation will see the African elephant.

iv

Table of Content

Acknowledgements.. vii

Preface.. ix

1. Social and Political Dimension of Environmental
Protection.. 1

2. Forest-Based Livelihoods and Sustainability Issues
In Unprotected Forests... 23

3. Population Dynamics, Livelihoods
And Forest Protection.. 45

4. Livelihoods and Threats to
Biodiversity Management.. 63

5. Rural Livelihoods and the
Management of National Parks... 83

6. Contribution of Non-Timber Forests Products
To Household Revenue in Forest-Adjacent Communities......................... 99

7. Forest-User Groups And Forest-Dependent
Livelihoods in Community Forests... 107

8. Gender Roles and Power Relationships
In Environmental Protection... 139

9. Ecological Planning and Ecotourism
Development in Protected Areas.. 157

10. Climate Change, Livelihoods
And Protected Area Management.. 175

11. Sustainable Forest Management by Communities......................... 203

Acknowledgements

The author is grateful for helpful and constructive comments on draft for this book from Professor C.M. Lambi, Dr. Z. Fogwe, Dr. C.A. Akob, and Professor N. R. Jeffers. Some of the case studies which they reviewed have previously been published in a different form. I am therefore grateful for the reproduction of some of the material from:

- Journal of Environmental Sciences, University of Jos, Nigeria.
- International Journal of Sustainable Development and World Ecology 14 (2007) 250 – 259, London.
- The Cameroon Geographical Review, the University of Yaounde, Cameroon.
- Journal of the Cameroon Academy of Sciences, University of Buea, Cameroon.
- International NGO Journal 4(5) May 2000, Academic Journals.
- Journal of Human Ecology, Kerela, India.

Special thanks go to Professor P. Utting and Professor G. Dharam for the material that constitutes the basis of the first chapter, that is, the social and political dimensions of environmental protection. The last chapter focuses on the participatory mapping methodologies for community forest management projects. It was realized thank to the work of Dr. Mike Nurse, Dr. Bill Jackson and Dr. H. Singh for the Rural Development Forestry Network (ODI, London).

The following students of the University of Yaounde I and University of Buea deserve special recognition for their contribution in the field phase of the case studies: E. Effange, Mgbe Selestin, Ichick Mbenga, Jai Julius, Y. Mbenmbem, K. Kemi, R. Fonyuy, M. J. Kwanga and Ndenecho Leslie. The conservator of the Kimbi Game Reserve and Staff of the Takamanda Forest Reserve also deserve special recognition.

The survey of Tubah Mountain Forest was realized thanks to the contribution of Rolf Boiler, Kum Sylvester and Ernestine Yende. The ethnobotanical data for Oku Mountain Forest was realized thanks to Jai Julius and staff of the Kilum Mountain Forest Reserve. Data for the Takamanda Forest Reserve is attributed to the contribution of T.C. Sunderland, Schmidt-Soltan, Tchouto and Mgbe Selestin.

The photographs documented in this book are reproduced from publications of the National Geographic (Special Publication for the 25th

Anniversary), Washington D.C.; and Mountain Research and Development, Berne (Switzerland).

Insights into the problems documented in the book are also the result of my consultancy work with local non-governmental organizations and International funding agencies such as the Swiss Association for Technical Cooperation (Helvetas) and the Netherland Development Organisation (SNV). I acknowledge with thanks my interaction with their projects in Cameroon. Finally, I acknowledge the encouragement of my teachers, students and family.

Preface

Tropical forest of Africa constitute nearly a fifth of the world's remaining forest. The forest is the home to numerous plants and animals. It is also inhabited by Baka pygmies who are foragers and Bantu farmers. The Baka are hunter-gatherers. They sometimes cultivate staple crops or trade agricultural work and forest products such as medicinal plants, "bush meat", medicinal plants, spices, edible vegetables, fruits, roots and tubers, mushrooms and honey, for commodities they could not otherwise obtain. Despite their gradual integration into mainstream society, they still possess many of their old ways, reaping from the forest a rich bounty. Forests from time immemorial have provided sustenance to forest dwellers and forest-adjacent communities. These communities have therefore developed forest – dependent livelihoods, cultures and religions.

It is becoming clear that tropical forest is not just a place apart, albeit a most astonishing complicated, extraordinary place. It is a world, too, of commerce and trade. This world takes form in transactions as simple as our exchange for honey or mushrooms on the porch and as intricate as the international market in mahogany logs. The destruction of tropical forests by commercial and state interests, subsistence agriculture and the harvesting of products is alarming. This has necessitated a considerable upsurge in environmental protection projects to conserve and rehabilitate ecosystems, forests, soil and water resources. Ultimately, the approach to conservation that is applied is the responsibility of the government and international development agencies. There is no reason why a Baka hunter or Bantu farmer should favour the protection of wildebeest and plants, just because the government and western opinion thinks he should. Indigenous people have evolved livelihoods and cultures that are supported by forests. The diverse complex interactions between people and the environment have often been ignored by conservation programmes and projects. This has resulted in livelihoods being negatively affected by protection projects. Consequently, local people respond in ways involving conflicts, illegal activities or "apathy" and "non-cooperation", which make programme / project implementation extremely difficult. The case studies documented in this book seek to demonstrate that a broader perspective linking environmental protection and human welfare is important for two reasons. First, it addresses the rights and needs of local people and more marginal groups in society. Second, it also ensures that fundamental conservation objectives are achieved in practice with the participation of local people.

The book therefore uses case studies to develop guidelines for a more integrative and socially – aware approach to environmental planning and project design and implementation. Forest protection projects which ignore their human neighbours are doomed to fail. There is a need for the trade-off between protection and human welfare. The environmental protection drive in Sub-Saharan Africa has gathered considerable momentum over the past decades. Unfortunately, there is still a wide gulf between government policy objectives and rhetoric, on the one hand, and the reality of policy and project implementation on the other. Measures aimed to protect the environment often impinge negatively on the livelihood of local people. The book emphasizes that at the local level, it is necessary to promote appropriate alternatives for local populations whose livelihoods are threatened by forest protection projects. There has been a tendency to focus attention exclusively on protected areas and to disregard the social, economic, cultural and land tenure situation of people in adjacent areas. Insufficient attention has been paid on how to integrate protected areas and local inhabitants. The book therefore outlines a participatory mapping procedure for the design and implementation of community forest programmes.

The book is multi-disciplinary. Based on the objectives outlined above, the book seeks to integrate the bio-physical, ecological, social, cultural, economic and political factors of sustainable development in the context of the effective and efficient design, and implementation of forest conservation projects in traditional societies. It is therefore a valuable book for land resource managers, environmentalists, environmental biologists, conservators, field workers and technicians involved with environmental conservation. With the professionalisation of courses in most universities, the book will constitute good reading for students of geography, biology, agriculture, forestry, botany and Natural Resource Management.

Emmanuel Neba Ndenecho

2011

Chapter 1

Social and Political Dimension of Environmental Protection

Summary

This study makes a critical examination of mainstream initiatives to protect and rehabilitate the environment in developing countries. It investigates the social dimensions of environmental degradation and regeneration, that is, the diverse and complex interactions between people and the environment. It thus seeks to integrate the physical and ecological with social, economic and political processes. It highlights these themes which emanate from case studies documented in the book. To achieve their objectives, the case studies employed an integrated and multidisciplinary approach to the analysis of environmental problems. In view of the paucity of information on the linkages between the ecological and social processes at grass root level, emphasis was put on the collection of original data through field research. The conclusion is that environmental protection schemes have not been effectively implemented and have even contributed to further degradation, social inequality and impoverishment. It is argued that the trade-off between protection and human welfare undermines not only local livelihoods but also the possibility of achieving basic environmental objectives, given the nature of local responses and their effects on project implementation. There is a need for a more integrative and socially-aware approach to planning which integrates concerns for environmental protection with the needs and rights of local people.

Key Words: Conservation policies, local people, livelihoods, indigenous knowledge, conflicts, Human welfare, sustainable development.

Introduction

It has now become evident that environmental protection projects in developing countries exhibit several micro-incoherencies. There is need for a critical appraisal of mainstream efforts to protect and rehabilitate the environment in Africa. Despite notable successes, many forest protection and tree planting schemes have not been effectively implemented, and have even contributed to further environmental degradation, social inequality and impoverishment. Despite the management problems there is a considerable upsurge in environmental protection projects to conserve and rehabilitate ecosystems, forests, soils and water resources. The concrete experience of policy, programme and project implementation in the field of environment protection, however, has raised serious doubts over the capacity of such schemes to contribute to sustainable development in general and human welfare in particular (Utting, 1994).

Most of the literature on the environment has focused on physical, ecological and economic aspects. There is a need to study the diverse and complex interactions between people and the environment, that is, to seek to integrate the physical and the ecological with social, economic and political processes. To achieve this objective, this study assumes an integrated and multi-disciplinary approach to the analysis of environmental problems. At the same, in view of the paucity of data on the linkages between the ecological and social processes at the local level, emphasis has been put on the collection of original data through field research.

The stress on social and political economy dimensions which underscores this study emanates from the conviction that programmes and protection projects concerned with conservation and sustainable development will only succeed on any scale when they address the social factors influencing the way local people interact with their environment (Dharam, 1994). These factors include access to employment, and essential resources such as land, credit, food, property systems and other key production resources associated with land, water, trees, gender relations and the question of empowerment. The case studies documented in this book reflect the research approach and themes outlined above. They draw upon original data in addressing the central question of how ecological changes interact with livelihood strategies, property regimes, gender roles and power relationships under specific social and environmental conditions. This way of looking at the environment yields fresh insights on such familiar themes as poverty, marginalization, subordination of women, social conflicts, popular resistance and mental regeneration. The conclusions point to the need to integrate into protection projects the knowledge and experience of local people. The central argument of the case studies is that as the drive to conserve and rehabilitate the environment gathers momentum it is crucial to focus more on the trade-off between environmental protection and human welfare. When environmental protection projects affect livelihoods negatively local people often respond in ways involving conflicts, illegal activities or "apathy" and "non-cooperation", which make programme or project implementation extremely difficult. It is argued, therefore, that a broader perspective linking environmental protection and human welfare is important, not simply from the obvious reason that it addresses the rights and needs of more marginal groups in society, but also to ensure that fundamental conservation objectives are achieved in practice.

Environmental Protection and Human Welfare

To minimize the trade-off between environmental protection and human welfare, it is crucial to address two basic problems that often affect ecological planning (Utting, 1994):

- The failure to locate environmental protection initiatives within a coherent development policy framework – what might be called a problem of macro-coherency; and
- The failure to integrate concerns of environmental protection with those relating to rights, needs, and priorities of local people – what might be called a problem of micro-coherency.

There has been a tendency to analyse the failure of many environmental protection projects largely in terms of technical, administrative and financial constraints or the limited environmental commitment or awareness of policy makers and natural resource users. The problem is often reduced to inadequate planning procedures which adopt short-term horizons for problems requiring long-term solutions, which do not consult with local people, or establish an appropriate framework for inter-agency coordination, or appropriate methods of technology diffusion which fail to convince the local natural resource user of the need to adapt his or her practices.

A more integrative and socially-aware approach to environmental planning and project design and implementation which addresses the two problems of "Coherency" noted above will not come about solely on the basis of increased awareness, availability of resources or technical know-how. Changes in the balance of social forces are also required. Especially important is the capacity of local people and, in particular disadvantaged groups to form themselves into constituencies which are able to demand accountability from local and national leaders and exert pressure for change. Also important is the role played by environmental social organization or "movements" in exerting influence on the policy process and applying pressures which can alter patterns of resource use and allocation by state and development agencies.

Recent Initiatives in Environmental Protection

A seemingly positive aspect of development process and strategies over the past three decades has been the considerable upsurge in environmental protection and the rehabilitation of plant, soil, animal and water resources. These decades have witnessed a flurry of activity on the part of the government of Cameroon, international non-governmental organizations (NGOs) and national NGOs aimed at designing and implementing policies, programmes and projects to conserve forests and encourage tree-planting. Despite the numerous constraints which characterize such projects, there have been some achievements. The number of officially declared national parks and protected areas has increased. The amount of land under protected area status has also increased. The government has also introduced generous fiscal incentive schemes to promote reforestation and community forestry. There has also been a large increase in the number of agroforestry and social forestry projects being implemented. Moreover, considerable resources have been channeled by the government and international funding agencies towards research and experimentation on agroforestry systems, forest resource surveys and inventories and silvopastoral research. Most of these initiatives have focused on the physical, ecological and economic aspects of environmental protection. Questions of livelihood procurement, the access of local people to key production resources, local knowledge and experiences are yet to be fully integrated in programmes and projects.

Photo: Baka Pygmies attuned to the forest rely on nets fashioned from vines to trap animals.

Photo: In the rainforest area, a girl dispels darkness in the traditional way: burning gum from a local tree. Oils from tropical plants may become more widely used as sources of energy.

Photo: Official shows elephant tusks confiscated from poachers: Ranger patrols and policing of protected areas affect local livelihoods negatively. Local people often respond in ways involving conflicts, illegal activities and non-cooperation.

Ecology, Gender and Property

There is a growing recognition at the level of research and rhetoric of the centrality of gender and property in the process associated with environmental degradation. But it is difficult to find many examples of actual policies and programmes for development and environmental protection which incorporate the results of these findings. There is by now a widespread understanding that, in their role as managers of natural resources, women have a key influence on the quality of the environment. It is also widely accepted that women and girls are affected by resource degradation both directly because of declining yields in agriculture and livestock and indirectly through increased workload in fetching water and fuel wood. Some of these issues are examined in the book.

Oppression and Resistance

Throughout history, the competition for natural resources has been a fertile ground for conflicts. In many rural areas of developing countries the struggle for the possession of natural resources has become a major cause of social conflicts. These have further been intensified by growing demographic pressures, shrinking economic opportunities and increasing concentration and scarcity of resources. Since the 1940s, the non-recognition in Cameroon of the customary rights of indigenous peoples to land and forests as a result of the creation of forest reserves has generated conflicts. In some cases it has resulted in the displacement and expulsion of indigenous people, reduction in available resources, insecurity in land and forest tenure. The consequence has been the impoverishment of local people and degradation of resources.

Only a restoration of land rights and autonomy in resource management to the tribal minorities can bring about a reversal of these negative trends. The forest-adjacent communities not only possess the knowledge for sound ecological management of their resources but have also shown evidence of their ability to accept changes and adapt to new circumstances. However, despite the resistance put by local communities to encroachment on their rights, which has resulted in some positive state initiatives to grant them ownership through community forestry, the processes of dispossession, impoverishment and ecological degradation continue apace. The forest protection projects littered over the country have in most instances resulted in uneven distribution of benefits, increasing inequalities in access to local resources and impoverishment of some sections of the population. These results are often attributed to demographic pressure, growing number of landless people and unemployment. The case studies documented in this book point to the fact that, impoverishment and marginalization are rather the result of primitive forms of seizure of the assets of certain minority groups by state interests. The current patterns of development are seen as resulting not only in ecological devastation but also in violation of property rights, displacement of local people, and loss of means of livelihood. Indeed, they threaten the very culture and way of life of entire communities.

Conservation and Development

Official conservation programmes have been motivated for the most part by the desire to attract foreign funds or to preserve scenic beauty, flora and fauna:

- There are projects which seek to protect forests, parks, animals and plant species for the benefit of present and future generations; and
- Projects which seek to rehabilitate and improve degraded resources to meet the subsistence needs of farmers, herders and foragers.

The record of the above projects is dismal. Forest protection projects have suffered because they have not only largely ignored the needs of local inhabitants and the communities in the neighbourhood of parks and protected areas, but in many cases have actually deprived them of means of subsistence through expulsion or restrictions on their access to land, forests, fisheries and grazing. It is the height of irony that conservation of resources of nature should result in the destruction of means of sustenance of people.

Climate Change Stresses and Human Welfare

Ayonghe (2001) showed that the net trend per decade in Cameroon based on data between 1930 and 2000 is a temperature increase of 0.14^{0}C. The highest rates of temperature increase per decade were at Banyo (0.24^{0}C), Maroua (0.23^{0}C), Kribi (0.32^{0}C) and Bertoua (0.21^{0}C). The lowest rates were at Ngaoundere (0.06^{0}C) and Mamfe (0.04^{0}C). In the same study plots of total amount of rainfall monitored at 11 stations showed decreasing trends in 6 stations. High rainfall was evident from 1951 to 1967, 1977 to 1980, and 1989 to 1995, while low rainfall was observed from 1930 to 1950, 1968 to 1976, and 1981 to 1988. In the drier regions of North Cameroon the data between 1960 and 1990 were in agreement with similar studies in the north-eastern arid zone of Nigeria where Carter and Alkali (1996) reported rainfall as decreasing by 8mm per year. The net changes in temperature across the entire country from 1930 to 1935 were 0.91^0C, which is equivalent to 0.14^0C per decade. Similarly, the net change in the total amount of rainfall was minus 282mm, equivalent to minus 43mm per decade. The net change in the annual number of rainy days was minus 7 days over the same period. When projected to the year 2060, these net changes give a temperature increase of 1.8^0C and rainfall decrease of 559mm, and 16 days respectively. The changes in mean number of rainy days are presented in table 1.

Table 1: Mean total number of rainy days computed from trend lines

Stations	1940	1960	1980	1995	2030	2060
Garoua	82.1	79.7	77.2	75.4	71.1	67.4
Ngaoundere	145.9	146.8	147.7	148.4	150.0	151.3
Mamfe	248.4	222.4	196.5	177.0	131.5	92.6
Bamenda	213.5	204.3	195.0	188.0	171.8	157.9
Banyo	138.4	151.6	164.9	174.8	198.0	217.8
Maroua	72.8	71.8	70.8	70.1	68.4	66.9
Douala	142.8	229.6	216.3	206.4	183.3	163.4
Kribi	209.0	205.1	201.1	198.2	191.3	185.4
Yaounde	148.9	149.1	150.5	151.2	152.9	154.3
Ebolowa	156.4	163.8	171.2	176.8	189.7	200.9
Bertoua	123.1	127.4	131.8	135.0	142.6	149.1
Mean	**161.9**	**159.1**	**156.6**	**154.7**	**150.0**	**146.1**

Source: Ayonghe, 2001

The effects of global warming on air and water temperatures are likely to be far more complicated than a gradual increase in average air temperatures. Both observational studies and models of future climate change suggest that there will be more variable temperatures, a greater frequency of extreme temperature events and more hot dry season days. They also predict a change in rainfall variability and an increase in the frequency of extreme rainfall due to an increase in the intensity of tropical storms. These will result in increased droughts and floods.

The weather and climate institutions of Cameroon, research institutes and universities should be updated by installing more conventional and upper air stations in the country so that their capacity for generating climatic data will be enhanced. This is necessary for climate projections and the sustainable management of natural systems. A National Climate Programme (NCP) should be launched in Cameroon geared towards human and institutional capacity building in climate change studies. This should be affiliated to similar programmes worldwide. Such institutes will generate climate data that will fashion government policy in the management of natural systems.

Climate change has a wide range of effects on biodiversity. As plants and animals rely on specific environmental conditions, changes in temperature and humidity regimes affect the performance and competiveness and relationships of species. Species adapted to cold conditions retreat to higher altitudes and latitudes while species living in warm areas may expand their ranges of distribution. This can cause problems if species expand that are regarded as pests, or if invasive species do harm to locally adapt ecosystems. The desert locust is an example, a slight increase in precipitation in susceptible areas in Africa where this insect lives may cause increased population densities. However, shifts in distribution areas will not always be possible as species may not be able to migrate through a landscape which has been increasingly fragmented by human activities. They may not also find a new place to establish as climate regimes do not fit or land use is inadequate. Consequently, climate change would be expected to further increase the global rate of species extinction.

The rapid change of environmental conditions is of particular concern for some hotspots of species diversity in Africa. These areas could transform from tropical forests to a Savannah-like formation. These areas will them lose large numbers of species, many of which are still unknown. These species form part of the living library needed to detect new pharmacological or crop species. On a single plant species level, climate change impacts on plant's phenology, that is, the time of the year when it starts flowering, develops fruits or dies. In Sub-Saharan Africa, the increased variability of precipitation might decrease the number of plant generations per year. In many areas, increasing temperatures are combined with a decreasing or at least more variable supply of water.

Another climate change related impact described is the potential "fertilization effect" of increased atmospheric CO_2. Many plants are limited in their growth by CO_2; therefore increased supply may lead to increased biomass accumulation or enhanced phenology development – as long as water and other nutrients are not limiting. In principle this is true for crops, too, but recent research results indicate that the delivery value of some crops might be reduced as the supplementary CO_2 leads to more sugar instead of proteins.

Decreasing biodiversity may be related to reduced food security as varying conditions cannot always be buffered by genetic or species diversity. The risk of famine increases with climate change, particularly when farming systems and livelihood options rely on few or only one species and institutions cannot provide support. Clearing mountain forest reduces the water storage functionality in catchments. In combination with floods and droughts induced by climate change, people suffer from erosion and water depletion.

The problems presented by climate related impacts are challenges for rural development and poverty alleviation. The biggest challenge is to tackle increasing rainfall variability, that is, the problem of droughts and floods combined with the overall loss of biodiversity. These are not only caused by climate change. Key areas for adaptation to climate change include;

- The design of guidelines for bioenergy production: rural areas in Sub-Saharan Africa face a new period of agricultural intensification for a rapidly growing population and the production of biomass for energy. In order to safe forest refugia bioenergy production might support rural development and maintain biodiversity on a small scale, especially on a farmer-scale.
- Protection of forest and trees. One of the key roles of vegetation with respect to climate change is to buffer against increasing temperatures. Respiration of forest enhances the cooling of the surrounding area and may even increase the probability of precipitation. The delineation of areas of for protection forests should have the following considerations.
- Delineation of montane forest areas for protection above 900m elevations for capturing sub-montane and montane forest habitats and subalphine communities.
- Delineation of protection forest in the lower elevations in order to capture elevational migration of species as well as transitional zones that appear to be crucial components of speciation and of the development of endemism.
- The development of agroforestry systems: This should seek to combine biodiversity conservation and climate change adaptation. Agroforestry systems are more resilient against climate change than treeless fields, as the trees reduce wind speed and therefore evaporation, and trap water and nutrients. They also harbour higher species diversity including predators that check insect pests.
- Enhancement of genetic crop diversity: This involves the development of a high agro-biodiversity which allows for local adaptation processes. It will require that farmers be supported in maintaining their locally adapted native varieties as an insurance against future increases of temperature variation and the occurrence of new pest and diseases.
- Development and promotion of soil and water conservation strategies: Soil tillage in combination with high temperatures leads to a rapid oxidation and loss of soil carbon. Organic farming and soil conservation

practices such as mulching or zero tillage enhance both the soil biological diversity, its fauna and also reduce carbon losses from the soil. Paying attention to the conservation of soils will permit a more sustainable agriculture to face climate change.

- Promotion of biodiversity governance at the global, regional and national levels. Biodiversity governance must be an intrinsic part of international and national legislation. Protected areas as a means to conserve the library for future crops and pharmacological development as well as retreat areas for plants and animals must be supported by international funding and trading mechanisms.

Nature conservation funds and "payments for ecosystem services" in Sub-Saharan Africa should be a global task; it should not be regarded as the responsibilities of the countries concerned. Such payments should encourage private land users to introduce environmentally friendly land use practices. The aim is to ensure that sustainable land resource management and conservation apply not only to specially designated protected areas, but also on productive land. The concept is based on the innovative idea of making payments for ecosystem services. This is particularly important because Sub-Saharan Africa faces additional challenges such as poverty and livelihoods sustenance:

The Trade-Off between Environmental Protection and Human Welfare

Environmental protection drive has gathered considerable momentum in Cameroon over the past decades. But there is still a wide gulf between government policy objectives and rhetoric, on the one hand, and the reality of policy and project implementation on the other. The Forestry Law of 1994 and many environmental laws remain unenforced, programmes or projects poorly implemented, while measures aimed to protect or rehabilitate the environment often impinge negatively on local people's livelihoods. The experiences of tree planting and forest protection programmes and projects reveal the following:

- The piece meal and partial character, or non-implementation, of many policies and programmes, as well as the difficulties of sustaining positive initiatives through time and replicating successful interventions;
- Many policies and schemes which attempt to control the use of forests give insufficient attention to the socio-economic and cultural situation of local people whose livelihoods depend on the resources of the forest;

- Schemes to promote tree planting often ignore not only the pressing need of the rural poor for basic food supplies, but also the complex and heterogeneous nature of the livelihood system of local land users;
- Fiscal and credit incentives, direct subsidies support services and other resources associated with many schemes are distributed unevenly, often appropriated by government agents or local elites, while the situation of weaker groups may deteriorate even further;
- Attempts by state or development agencies to protect or rehabilitate the environment in one area are often contradicted by other "development" measures which degrade the environment.

Integrating Environmental and Livelihood Concerns

At the local level, it is necessary to promote appropriate alternatives for local populations whose livelihoods are threatened by environmental rehabilitation initiatives. This is particularly relevant in the case of protected area schemes which displace people or impose restriction on their traditional subsistence provisioning and economic activities. Moreover, there has been a tendency to focus attention exclusively on protected areas and to disregard the social, economic, cultural and land tenure situation of people in adjacent areas. Insufficient attention has often been paid to the development of buffer zones and the question of how to integrate parks and local inhabitants.

Conservation initiatives which minimize the trade-off between environmental protection and human welfare must involve intensive dialogue with various local groups in the design stage of forest protection or tree planting programmes and projects. Conservation schemes must also attempt to build upon, rather than ignore, the existing stock of local knowledge regarding natural resources and resource management systems.

There has been little assessment of the social impact of government or agency schemes which alter agricultural land use patterns by encouraging producers to plant trees, or attempt to take large tracts of land out of traditional exploitation by establishing protected area zones. Social impact assessments (SIAs) would need to:

- Determine which social groups stand to win or lose from a specific project;
- Identify potential conflicts of interest and examine procedures for resolving them;

- Consider how local populations might respond when their livelihoods or interest are affected as well as the social and environmental implications of such responses; and
- Explore alternative livelihood scenarios for individuals and groups affected by such schemes.

This broader perspective linking environmental and human welfare is important, not only for the obvious reason that it addresses the rights and needs of more marginal groups in society, but also to ensure that fundamental conservation objectives can be achieved in practice. In most instances, where social conflicts arise in protected area management, the state often has chosen not to implement the law rather than add fuel to fire. Hence non-implementation of protected area status often constitutes the means by which to resolve conflicts.

Most protected areas are in isolated, remote locations. People in such outlying forest areas have often been subjected to isolation and marginality. Establishing protected areas is an extremely complex undertaking not only because it involves fundamental changes in land use practices and human settlement patterns but also because it involves extending the arm of the state and development agencies into areas where suspicion of such agents, or overt opposition, is likely to characterize the attitudes of local people. Social groups living in remote areas are probably amongst those least willing to cooperate with the latest development fad, however ecologically sound it happens to be. Such situations require serious consideration by project planners for they raise important questions about the feasibility of protected area schemes, the possibilities and mechanics of dialogue, types of regulation or incentives, levels of compensation, and so forth.

Mauambeta (1999) identified the root causes of forest degradation in rural Malawi as being poverty and ignorance. A related study in Tanzania (Iddi, 1998) reported dense population and encroachment into forest by farming as main challenges facing forest management. A World Bank study (2002) in India associated forest degradation with poverty, agricultural pressure, intensive grazing and fuel wood collection. Similar studies in Nigeria (Bisong, 1998) establish agricultural land use pressure, unsustainable harvesting of timber products and non-timber forest products, widespread poverty, population growth and inadequate government policy as the main causes of forest degradation and the failure of forest protection projects. These studies point to the need to integrate rural livelihoods in protected area management projects, that is, the need to research for forms of participatory forest management (Dudley *et al*; 1994). This management approach involves all the collective or individual activities and practices centred on trees and forests, and carried out by local communities for the sustainable satisfaction of their needs (Bigombe, 1999). According to WRI (2005) this definition is limited to the management of forests by rural people based on their indigenous knowledge base, social, cultural and economic links. It ignores policies and laws that integrate the forest management processes, social considerations, and issues of sustainability and stakeholder - participation. Carter and Gronow (2005) have therefore defined participatory forest management as "a working partnership between the key stakeholders in the management of a given forest."

Participatory forest management differs from region to region, depending on tenure system, policy, legislature environment as well as the state of the forest being managed. Domodaran (2003) defines it as a partnership between the local communities (villages) and the state forest department (government) in which management responsibilities and benefits of products are shared. But the forest department retains control over the partnership. Carter and Gronow (2005) however point out that partnerships between the government and local communities in forest management always result in conflicts in management policies and the sharing of benefits. They therefore introduced a third party mediator, that is, the private sector represented by nongovernmental organizations (NGOs) and termed the approach collaborative forestry management in which no one stakeholder takes full control of strategic and sometimes operational management. (Mc Dougall *et al*; 2007) emphasized that in collaborative forestry management there is need for stakeholders to adapt to uncertainty and complexity in sharing management power and responsibility of forest, hence Adaptive Collaborative Forest Management. They identified the sources of uncertainties as: changes in livelihoods, changes in social relations and changes in government policies.

Bamberger (1988) conceptualized and defined participatory forest Management as an evolutionary process in which activities at the project or micro-level can create the conditions for increased popular participation in the planning and implementation of development programmes at local, regional and national levels. Six elements are adopted as yard stick for making a comparative analysis of various participatory forest management approaches:

- Organizations and groups involved or instruments;
- Project implementation methods;
- Stages of the project in which the beneficiaries are involved;
- Scope of the programme;

- Participants; and
- Intensity of participation.

Organizations and groups involved include workers of the project; who are either paid or provide voluntary services. The methods of implementation vary from formal leadership training programmes to learning by doing through the implementation of projects whereby communities are helped to understand their own needs and to identify possible solutions. Stakeholder participation in decision-making and implementation of social, political, cultural mechanisms to enforce management regulations are crucial to the success of community forest Management. These are necessary aspects to consider in the evaluation of activities and outcomes or outputs of the project. The scope of the programmes may vary from the micro-levels, district, regional and national levels, with some involving several projects. The participants include, all stakeholders (men and women) and the poor or marginalized, who have generally been overlooked. Finally, stakeholder-participation includes information sharing, consultation, decision-making and determining the intensity of involvement of local communities.

Paul (1987) outlines the objectives of Participatory forest management:

- Sharing project cost; beneficiaries contribute in kind or cash;
- Increasing project efficiency; through consultation during project planning and involvement of local people in project implementation;
- Increasing project effectiveness, by helping the project achieve its objectives and by ensuring that benefits accrue to the intended groups;
- Building beneficiary capacity, through stakeholder-participation in project conception, planning, implementation, monitoring and evaluation; and
- Increasing empowerment, that is, increasing the control of the underprivileged groups of the community over resources and decisions affecting the sustainability of their livelihoods.

Essentially, participatory forest management should address livelihood concerns. Forest - adjacent communities should be able to move from position as subordinate beneficiaries to regulate their resources of livelihood with a longer-term perspective. They should be able to assist in securing tenure rights, by identifying and placing under local jurisdiction socio-spatial boundaries, encourage democratization through grassroots participation, and good governance in conservation and protected area management (Alden, 2003).

Drawing from the above objectives (Paul, 1987) outlined the benefits of community forest management:

- Sharing of forest access or sharing of benefits: buffer zone development, agro-forestry, employment opportunities (local livelihood sustenance) and legalizing of local forest use;
- Sharing of authority over forest resources or power sharing through the use of local socio-political mechanisms to regulate forest resource exploitation and management. This involves the devolvement of management decisions or managerial control to the community:
  - Relocation of management as near the resource as possible;
  - Transfer of jurisdiction to those having vested interest in the forest environment for their survival and for socio-ritual and customary reasons;
  - Ensuring the sustainability of local livelihoods and therefore the forest ecosystem as a result of vested interests;
  - Building up of local custodial interest and tenure; and
  - Empowerment of local community and stakeholders; and promote the validation of indigenous knowledge.

Scoones (1998) defines local livelihoods as the capabilities, assets (both material and social resources) and activities required for a means of living. These are the ways in which people satisfy their needs or gain a living. The sustainability of livelihoods is the ability to maintain and improve livelihoods while maintaining or enhancing the asset on which livelihoods depend (Chambers and Conway, 1992). Livelihood systems display varying degrees of sustainability and resilience and their sustainability is determined by the outcomes of those interactions and changes imposed on them by human action and exogenous events (Maxwell and Smith, 1988). Figure 1 presents the Sustainable Rural Livelihood framework. It starts with the vulnerability context within which rural people operate. Vulnerability refers to forces outside rural people's control; and includes shocks, trends and seasonalities (DFID, 2000). Livelihood resources or assets are those activities on which people build their livelihoods. These include N = natural capital, F = financial capital, P = physical capital, S = social capital and H = human capital.

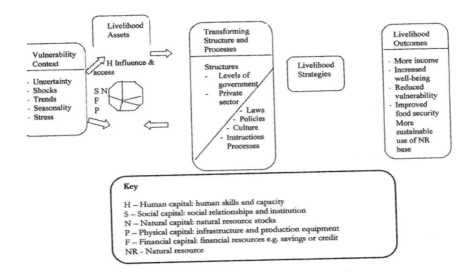

Figure 1: Sustainable Rural Livelihood Framework (DFID, 200)

Structure and processes in the model implies the means by which rural people gain access to assets in pursuit of different livelihood strategies. Livelihood choice strategies are choices people employ in pursuit of income, security, well-being and other productive and reproductive goals. The livelihood outcomes indicate the extent to which rural welfare has improved in a sustainable way such as poverty reduction, increased food security, and greater resilience. The outcomes can have feedback effects on the vulnerability status and the resource base.

The above framework explains the sustainability of a rural livelihood. A livelihood is sustainable, if it can cope with and recover from stress and shocks, maintaining or enhancing its capabilities and assets, provide a net benefit to other livelihoods both now and in future, without undermining the natural resource base. A key step in analyzing rural livelihood sustainability is to identify what livelihood resources are required for different strategies. In sustaining rural livelihood, local people develop strategies. These may have either positive or negative effects on the resource base. If negative effects occur the consequence is a diminishing wellbeing. These negative effects intensify the extent of the degradation of the asset or resource because scarcities induce the need to capture more resources directly and indirectly through the diversification of livelihood activities. Furthermore, when the resource base can no longer sustain rural livelihoods rural people migrate to towns in search of unskilled jobs. Their remittances offset stresses and shocks back in the rural community. The outcomes assess the extent to which human wellbeing has been improved, for instance, creating employment with good incomes and poverty reduction. From the framework, rural livelihood sustainability is secured by adapting to vulnerability, enhancing the resilience of the resource base to anthropic stresses, trends, seasonality and climate-change related stresses; and also enhancing the conservation of the resource base (Livelihood assets).

The Cameroon forestry law of 1995 is the main legal instrument to implement community forest management in the country. Community-based management of natural resources originates from the second objective of the forestry policy which aims at "enhancing the participation of the populations in the conservation and management of forests, in order to contribute in improving their living standards." The case studies documented in this book seek to develop guidelines for a more integrative and socially – aware approach to environmental planning and project design and implementation. It appraises the current management strategies and identifies the scope for the integration of local livelihood concerns in protected area management.

Conclusion

A social perspective on the environment, as opposed to one based purely on ecology or technology, shows that the issues of resource degradation and regeneration are intimately linked to questions of power, institutions, livelihood and culture. There is a need for a more integrative and socially-aware approach to environmental planning and project design. The case studies documented in this book indicate that progress on the environmental front depends to a large extent on whether or not basic livelihoods issues are addressed. Conservation policies and schemes which fail to balance environmental protection and human welfare are likely to result not only in increased hardship for certain social groups but also in forms of social conflict, clandestine activities, non-cooperation or apathy which undermine the possibility of effectively arresting environmental degradation, let alone rehabilitating the natural resource base. Thus, conservation schemes should enhance the livelihood security of local communities, *inter alia*, through recognition of their customary rights over natural resources. The success of such efforts depends on their ability to strengthen the technical, organizational and managerial capabilities of rural communities and organizations. The book highlights the importance of reinforcing local knowledge and innovative capacity, and the need to recognize the priorities, concerns and rights of women, especially their rights of access to key production resources. Conservation projects must also envisage the mitigation of adverse effects of climate change on biodiversity and the sustainability of livelihood activities.

References

Alden, L. W. (2003). Participatory Forest Management in Africa. An Overview of Progress and Issues, DFID.

Annis, S. (ed) (1992) Poverty, natural resources and public policy in Central America. New Brunswick, Transaction Publishers.

Amanor, K. (1992) Ecological knowledge and the regional economy: environmental management the Asesewa District of Ghana. UNRISD *Conference Paper on the Social Dimensions of Environment and Sustainable Development*, Valleta, Malta (22 – 25 April, 1992).

Ayonghe, S. (2001) A quantitative evaluation of global warming and precipitation in Cameroon from 1930 to 1995 and Projections to 2060: Effects on the environment and water resources. In: E.B. Eze and C.M. Lambi (eds). *Readings in Geography*, Unique publishers, Bamenda, p. 142 – 155.

Bamberger, M. (1988) The Role of Community Participation in Development Planning and Project Management. *Economic Development Institute, E.D.I.*, The World Bank, Washington D.C.

Berkes, F. (1997) New and not-so-new directions in the use of the commons: Co-management. *The Common Property Resource Digest.* 42: 5 – 7

Bisong, F.E. (1998) Three Model Community Participatory Forest Management in Cross River State. *Study Report prepared for the Forestry Development,* Cross River State, Nigeria.

Bigombe Logo, P. (1999). Participatory forest management, a strategy for sustainable forest management in Africa. *Proceedings of the International Workshop on Community Forestry in Africa: 26 – 30 April, 1999*, Banjul, the Gambia.

Bloch, P. (1992) Tenure issues in forest buffer zones. *Paper Presented at Seminar on Institutional Issues in Natural Resource Management in Africa.* Holback, Denmark (16th – 20th November).

Carter, R. and Alkali, A. (1996) Shallow groundwater in Northeastern arid zone of Nigeria. *Quarterly Journal of Engineering Geology, vol. 29*, p. 341 – 355.

Carter, J., Steenhof, B., Haldiman, E. and Akenshaev, N. (2003). Collaborative forest management in Kyrgyzstan: Moving from top down to bottom up decision making. *Gatekeeper series*, 108 IIED.

Carter, J. and Gronow, J. (2005). Recent Experience in collaborative forest management. *Occasional paper, N° 43*. A Review Paper, CIFOR 2005.

Chamber, R. and Conway, G. (1992). Sustainable livelihoods, environment and development: Putting poor rural people first. *IDS Discussion paper 20*.

Dharma, G. (1994) Environment, livelihood and empowerment. In: G. Dharam (ed). *Development and environment: sustaining people and nature*. Blackwell Publishers / UNRISD.

Department for International Development (2000). Sustainable Livelihoods guidance sheets DFID.

Dove, M.R. (1992) Joint Forest Management in India. *Report to Food Foundation*, New Delhi.

Dudley, N., J – P Jeanrenaud and S. Stolton (1994). Towards a definition of forest quality. WWF, UK, Godalming Survey.

Friedmann, J. and Rangan, H. (eds) (1993) In defense of livelihood: comparative studies in environmental action. Connecticut, Kumarian Press.

Houseal, B.; MacFarland, C.; Archibold, G. and Chiari, A. (1985) Indigenous cultures and protected areas in Central America. *Cultural Survival Quarterly*, March 10 – 20.

Iddi, S. (1998) Community involvement in forest management: First experiencefrom Tanzania. The Gologolo Joint Forest Management Project: A case study from the West Usambara Mountains. *Paper presented at workshop on Community Forest in Africa, 26 – 30 April, 1999*, Banjul, the Gambia.

Mauambeta, D.D.C. (1999) Sustainable management of indigenous forest in Mwanza East, Malawi: An innovative approach to community-based natural resource management projects. *Working paper on participatory forest management: A strategy for sustainable forest management in Africa, 26 – 30 April, 1999,* Banjul, the Gambia.

Maxwell, S. and Smith, M. (1998) Household Food Security: A ConceptualReview in S. Maxwell and T. Frankenberger (eds). *Household Food Security: Concepts, Indicators, Measurements.*

Mc-Dougall, C.; Kaski, ACM Team, New ERA-ACM Team and Forest Action (2005). Planning for the sustainability of forest through adaptive co-management: Nepal Country report. *ACM Project / MOFSC Internal Research Report,* CIFOR, Bogor.

Mc-Dougall, C., Pandit, B. H., Paude, K. P., Banjade, M., Paude, N. S., Maharjan, M., Rana, S., Bhattarai, T. and Dangol, S. (2007). Forest of learning: An adaptive collaborative management approach to community forest in Nepal. *A guidebook for facilitators at the community forest user group level.* CIFOR, Bogor.

MINEF (1998) Manual of the Procedure for the Attribution and Norms for the Management of Community Forest, Cameroon. Ministry of Environment and Forestry.

Paul, S. (1987) "Community Participation in Development Projects: The World Bank Experience." In: *Readings in Community Participation.* Washington D. C.; EDI, Chapter 2.

Scones, I. (1998) Sustainable Rural Livelihoods: A Framework for analysis. *IDS working paper, N° 27,* Brighton: IDS.

Utting, P. (1993) Trees, people and power. London: Earthscan Publication.

Utting, P. (1994) Social and political dimensions of environment protection in Central America. In: Dharam, G. (ed). *Development and environment: sustaining people and nature.* Blackwell Publishers / UNRISD.

World Bank (2002) Project Appraisal document: Andhra Pradesh Community Forest Management Project (P073094). *Report Nᵒ 24184.* World Bank, Washington D. C.

World Resources Institute (WRI) (2005). World Resources 2005: The Wealth of the Poor-Managing Ecosystems to fight poverty. Washington D. C.; WRI/UNDP/The World Bank.

Chapter 2

Forest Based Livelihoods and Sustainability Issues in Protected Areas

Case Study: Tubah Mountain Forest

Summary

The capacity of forests to provide sustainable employment opportunities is becoming the focus of greater interest worldwide. Unfortunately, research and information on forest-based livelihood and their effects on the sustainability of forests are limited at both local and national levels. The paper therefore, focuses on the effects of wood fuel consumption, overgrazing and subsistence farming on montane forests. It uses a combination of primary and secondary data sources to establish these effects in quantitative and qualitative terms and to investigate the underlying causes of deforestation. The chapter establishes that the root causes are diverse and require a more comprehensive and objective view of the problem. It identifies the rising fuel wood consumption as the principal cause of deforestation in the forest. Other causes include subsistence farming and overgrazing. These activities have adversely affected the boundaries of the forest. The chapter therefore, recommends the adoption of ecologically integrated land use management systems and the appreciation of the complex extremely dynamic and multi-sectoral issues underlying the broader crisis of population pressure, food security, energy acquisition, poverty and natural resource usage.

Introduction

The capacity of forests to provide sustainable employment opportunities is becoming the focus of greater interest worldwide (Soudan and Zingaré, 2000). In mountain areas, forest resources are a considerable source of livelihood and of multiple economic activities based on a variety of goods and services (Ndenecho, 2006). Although forest resources contribute greatly to livelihoods and to many economic activities through a great diversity of goods and services, research and information on forest-based livelihoods and forest-related employment are limited at both the local and national level (Poschen, 1997). In order to raise an awareness of the links between mountain forests, the forest based-informal sector and the sustainability of forests in developing countries, the chapter seeks to assess the effects of cultivation, cattle grazing and wood fuel consumption on the quality and quantity of montane forest environments.

Tubah Mountain Forest is part of the Cameroon Highlands ecoregion which comprises montane forest and grassland patches mainly above 900 m elevation. This ecoregion is scattered in an archipelago along the border area between Cameroon and Nigeria (Figure 1). Habitat ranges with increasing altitude from sub-montane to montane forests and ultimately sub-alpine grassland (Stuart, 1986). The montane forests are found within the 1800 and 2200 m elevation in the Bamenda-Banso Highlands. In the majority of cases, however, the lower boundary of these forests is now determined by conversion to agricultural land use.

The slopes range from flat and gentle sloping in the upland basins to very steep towards the ridges and downwards to streams. Rainfall varies from 1780 to 2290 mm per year and most rain falls between July and September. Generally January and February have the lowest relative humidity (averages 45 – 52%). The monthly average exceeds 80% in July and August. During the rainy season, mist and low cloud occur frequently. The dry season lasts from mid – November to mid – March when the dry season sets in. Mean maximum temperature is 20 to 22°C and the mean minimum 13 to 14°C. November has the lowest mean minimum and December the highest mean maximum.

According to Macleod (1986) these forests have one of the highest levels of endemism in the whole of Africa, particularly among birds and vascular plants (Bowden and Andrews, 1994 Dowsett, 1989 and Stuart, 1986). Despite their scientific importance, the montane forests of Cameroon have received little conservation attention.

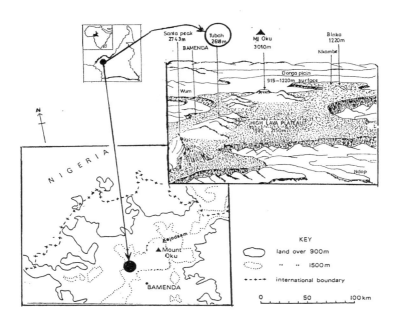

Figure 1: Location of the study area: Tubah Mountain Forest.

These forests were once widespread on the Bamenda-Banso plateau (Figure 1) and adjacent mountains but have been extremely cleared (Nkwi and Warnier, 1982; Morin, 1978; Dongmo, 1984, Kodomura, 1986; Zimmermann, 1994). The rich volcanic soils on which they grow are among the most fertile in the country (Hawkins and Brunt, 1965; Hoff et al, 1987). The area also has one of the highest population densities (Ngwa; 1979; Neba, 1999). The combination of these factors results in enormous pressure to clear the remaining forest for agriculture and grazing. In addition to their scientific interest, these highlands also form essential water catchments for Cameroon and Nigeria (Zimmermann, 1994). Forest loss has been significant in many mountains in the ecoregion. Much of the Bamenda-Banso Highlands were once totally covered with forest, but cover has declined by more than 50% since the 1960s through conversion for cultivation, because of the relatively fertile soils and reliable rainfall (Stuart, 1986; Collar and Stuart 1988; Alpert, 1993).

Research Methods

The study investigated the effects of cultivation, fuel wood collection and grazing on the extent of forest depletion between 1950 and 2000. A reconstruction of the extent of the forest in 1960 was done using the following maps:

- 1961 photographic reconnaissance of Bamenda area (Bawden and Langdale-Brown (1961).
- Map of West Cameroon at scale of 1/100.000 (National Geographic Institute, 1967).
- Map of Nkambe – Wum at a scale of 1/50.000 (National Geographic Institute, 1965).
- Soils and ecology of Cameroon: Map at a scale of 1/200.000 (Hawkins and Brunt, 1968).

These sources were complemented by the works of Kadomura (1984), Tamura (1986), Morin (1978) on the environmental geomorphology of the area. These enabled a mapping of the 1960 situation of the extent of the forest.

A land use map for the area was established for 2000 (Ndenecho, 2003) using a land use base map from the National Geographic Institute for 1987 and aerial photographs. These were updated by the use of a global positioning system to map the forest boundaries and other land use systems. After ground reconnaissance surveys, the 2000 land use map permitted the survey team to select forest sites for detailed study. A total of six plots were selected and the floristic composition, land use and volume of standing timber investigated.

The fieldwork was carried out with the assistance of a forestry technician and two agricultural technicians working in the area. With the background knowledge about the forest, sample plots were then selected by visual observation, when a plot was selected a central point with 10 m radius was established forming a circular plot. This was followed by:

- Measuring of distance and compass angle of each tree with a tape.
- Identification of species and the estimates of volume of stems and branches.
- Description of forest type and importance of fuel wood on the stand.

Identification and measurements were carried out on all trees enumerated as found within the circular plot. The measurements taken were:

- Distance of tree to plot centre.

- Distance between tree and measuring point of angle and circumference with the use of tapes.
- Total height of the tree and stem height measured indirectly using a "sunnto" clinometre.
- The direction of the tree to plot centre was measured using a compass while slopes were measured using an altimeter.

All tree measurements were for stem height determination, for volume computation of each tree species and plot volume of timber.

For each plot detailed information was collected on the following aspects:
- Situation of plot and accessibility.
- Land use/exploitation.
- Species composition, height and density of the forest.
- Evidence of recent forest fires and fuel wood collection or harvesting.

Measurements on trees respected the following rules:
- Measuring the circumference(c) at the height of 1.3 m.
- Measuring both stems if the fork of a tree is below 1.3 m height.
- Counting only trees with circumference larger than 31 cm or a 10 cm diameter (d).

$C = d \times \pi$ where $\pi = 3.14$.

The height of trees was estimated by the use of a clinometers. The following formulae were used for height measurement with clinometers.

TOTAL HEIGHT	$(B_3 - B_1) \times d \times$ cos a	Where B_1 = angle to bottom B_3 = angle to top crown a = slope angle of the ground d = distance between tree and person.
STEM HEIGHT	$(B_2 - B_1) \times d \times$ cos a	Where: B_1 = angle to bottom B_3 = angle to top crown a = slope angle of the ground d = distance between tree and person

Final volume calculations were made by employing the following formula:

$$V = \left(\pi \cdot \frac{D2 \cdot H}{4} \right)$$

Where: V = volume

H = Tree stem height

D = average diameter of tree of breast height i.e. 1.3m

$$= \quad 0.785398 \quad \frac{\pi}{4}$$

The volume of wood (m^3) per hectare of forest stand was established from the above calculations. Based on an average farm size of 8 persons and a monthly average fuel wood consumption of $3m^3$ the rate of deforestation was estimated in order to establish the final exhaustion time. Informal interviews of farmers and farm family heads yielded the local uses of trees and also identified the root causes and the effects of deforestation. These assisted in the elaboration of strategies for the sustainable management of land resources, and a strategy that can turn the tide towards the sustainability of wood fuels.

Results and Discussions

Table 1: Ethnobotanical survey of Tubah mountain forest

Scientific Name	Family Name	Local Uses
Acacia sp	*Mimosoideae*	Charcoal, Fencing, Firewood
Albizia coriara	*Mimosoideae*	Timber, Fencing, Charcoal, Firewood
Angaura salicifolia	*Ericaceae*	Highly medicinal
Bridelia speciosa	*Euphorbiaceae*	Local tooth brush production
Canarium schweifurthii	*Bursearaceae*	Fruits, shell, timber, medicinal
Cordia africana	*Boraginaceae*	Poles, carving, medicinal
Carapa grandifora	*Meliaceae*	Timber, poles
Croton macrost	*Euphorbiaceae*	Fencing, poles, timber, shade, medicinal
Entada abyssinica	*Mimosoideae*	Charcoal, poles, timber
Eucalyptus sp	*Wyrtaceae*	Timber, poles, fencing
Ficus sp	*Moraceae*	Shade, fencing, carving
Kigelia africana	*Bignoniaceae*	Carving, traditional
Cola allata	*Rubiaceae*	Medicinal, edible seeds
Lasiociphon glaucus	*Thymelaeceae*	Local production of papers and envelopes

28

Maespsis manii	/	Timber, shade, carving, medicinal
Newtonia buchananii	*Mosaceae*	Carving
Noubouldia laevis	*Bignoniaceae*	Timber, carving
Polyscia fulva	*Araliaceae*	Poles, timber, honey, charcoal
Schefflera abyssinica	*Araliaceae*	Timber, carving
Vitex diversifolia	*Verbenaceae*	Timber, carving
Vitex doniana	*Verbenaceae*	Edible fruits, carving
Voacanga sp	*Apocynaceae*	Seeds, medicinal, local and industrial poles, timber
Entandrophragma angolense	*Meliaceae*	Timber (furniture)
Trema orientalis	*Ulmaceae*	Medicinal value for women
Xailobier sp	/	Fire wood
Pittosporum manii	*Pittosporaceae*	Furniture, medicinal
Prunus africana	*Rosaceae*	Highly medicinal bark
Nuxia congesta	*Loganiaceae*	Musical instruments
Faraga rubescens	*Rutaceae*	Fuel wood
Khaya senegalensis	*Meliaceae*	Good timber
Raphia farinifera	*Palmae*	Fibre, handicraft, wine, construction bamboo, wood

Table 1 presents the results of the ethnobotanical survey. The study area has a population density of 100 inhabitants / km^2. According to the data projected from the 1987 National Population Census the population of the area was 18.891 inhabitants in 1998. At an estimated growth rate of 3.8% it was 24,527 inhabitants in 2005 and shall be 35,527 inhabitants in 2015. Several rural livelihoods therefore depend on the forest. The main livelihood activities provided by the forest are presented in table 1. These are mainly timber, poles, fuel wood and charcoal, and non-timber products. The ribonning growth of Bamenda city along the highway that traverses the villages and the forests if left unchecked will merge with Tubah. The area is sub-urban (8km from Bamenda city) and the urban and rural demands of timber and non-timber forest products are imposing biological stresses on the forest. Lack of alternative livelihood activities for a growing number of unemployed youths is one of the major causes of the accelerated degradation of the forest.

The main floristic and land use characteristics of six sample sites were investigated:

29

PLOT 1:

- **Altitude:** 2010 m and 2030 m above sea level.
- **Floristic composition:** *Lasiocephon glaucas, croton macrostachyus, Bridelia sp.* and *Nuxia sp.* with *Nuxia* being the dominant species. Generally an open wood with an open canopy. The undergrowth is composed of bracken fern, *Sporobolus africnas, Cedar circulata,* and *Aframumun sp. Sporobolus* is the dominant grass.
- **Land use:** site is partially used by graziers and was partially burnt to stimulate new growth for cattle. Signs of timber and fuel wood extraction were visible.

PLOT 2

- **Altitude:** 1910 m and 1930 m above sea level.
- **Floristic composition:** Trees include *Carapa grandifolia, Ficus oreodryadum, Canarium schweifurthii, Schefflera abyssinica, Newtonia buchananii* with *Carapa* and *Canarium* being dominants. This was a dense forest area with a close canopy, with shrubs, climbers, twigs and grasses interwoven, and forming a thicket. The forest floor was covered with dense litter, dead tree logs and branches, fresh and dry leaves. *Aframumum* and bracken fern were dominant undergrowth.
- **Land use:** Some timber and fuel wood extraction and signs of dry season bush fires on trees trunks.

PLOT 3

- **Altitude:** 1800 m above sea level.
- **Floristic composition:** Similar to plot 2, the dominant species was Carapa grandifolia.
- **Land use:** Some timber and fuel wood extraction and signs of dry season bush fires on tree trunks.
-

PLOT 4

- **Altitude:** 1840 to 1858 metres above sea level.
- **Floristic composition:** Hill slope was completely burnt by slash-and-burn cultivation. Signs of burning were concentrated on tree stumps, and the few trees found included *Croton, Albizia* and *Bridelia,* with *Bridelia* being the dominant species.

- **Land use:** There is evidence of slash-and-burn cultivation and fallow periods of 1 – 2 years which permit cattle to graze fallow vegetation. This is accompanied by annual bush fires and fuel wood and timber extraction is common.

PLOT 5

- **Altitude:** 1920 metres above sea level
- **Floristic composition:** Tall trees with a one canopy layer: *Albizia, Carapa,* and *Voacanga,* with *Voacanga* being the dominant species. The forest floor was clean (probably swept by bush fires).
- **Land use:** Plot accessible by cattle track close to a stream. Plot undergrowth probably degraded by grazing and bush fires during the dry season. Visible signs of fuel wood extraction and logging were present.

PLOT 6

- **Altitude:** 1020 m above sea level.
- **Floristic composition:** Trees included *Albizia, Carapa,* and *Voacanga,* with *Carapa* being the dominant species. Trees were very tall forming a one layer close canopy. The undergrowth was composed of *Aframumum,* bracken fern and *Sporobolus africanus.*
- **Land use:** Evidence of bush fires was visible on tree trunks and the undergrowth. Cattle tracks at the forest fringe were also indicative of some grazing. Fuel wood extraction and logging were also visible.

Wood is extracted for various purposes: charcoal, fencing, fuel wood, construction timber, poles, carving, tooth brush production, production of packaging bags, fabrication of musical instruments and bridges. The volume of wood in the remaining forest per sampled plot for the main tree species harvested by local people was estimated (Table 2).

Table 2: Volume tables per plot of each species

Species of trees	Volume per plot (m³)	Volume per hectare (m³)

PLOT 1

Species of trees	Volume per plot (m³)	Volume per hectare (m³)
Lasiociphon	1.49	47.422
Nuxia	1.78	56.652
Croton	0.5	15.913
Bridelia	1.43	45.512
Total	**5.2**	**165.499**

PLOT 2

Capara	3.42	108.848
Ficus	0.22	7.001
Canarium	3.35	106.62
Total	**6.99**	**222.469**

PLOT 3

Wink	13.7	436.028
Capara	3.7	117.759
Khaya	0.5	15.913
Unident	3.5	111.394
Total	**21.4**	**681.094**

PLOT 4

Croton	3.12	99.300
Bridelia	4.19	133.355
Albizia	6.33	210.464
Total	**13.64**	**434.119**

PLOT 5

Carapa	1.130	35.964
Unident	0.84	35.964
Newtonia	10.9	346.913
Birdelia	2.36	75.111
Total	**15.230**	**484.723**

PLOT 6

Albizia	4.52	143.857
Unident	.18	5.729
Capara	3.6	114.577
Voacanga	.03	.955
Total	**8.330**	**265.120**

Table 2 presents the volume of wood for each sampled plot per tree species frequently harvested for local uses. The original vegetation of sub-montane forest is fast disappearing. From field observations the dominant tree species include *Croton, Albizia, Trema, Ficus spp., Newtonia, Polyscia fulva, Combretum, Voacanga* and *Pygeum* africanus are medicinal plants are important commercial medicinal plants that have been degraded by poor harvesting techniques. A large variety of plants that form the forest undergrowth are destroyed by annual dry season bush fires set by farmers and graziers. Trees scorch at their bole and quickly dry up and die. The dead wood is subsequently harvested for fuel wood and timber. Based on the volume tables presented in table 2 a quantitative assessment of fuel wood consumption and deforestation rate was established (Table 3).

Table 3: Fuel wood indicators for Tubah communities

Grand Total Plot 1 – 6	2.253.024 m³
Average volume per hectare	375.504 m³
Standing volume for Tubah forest (500 ha)	187.752.000 m³
No. of farm families in Tubah (1998)	2.362 families
Average fuel wood requirements/month/family	3.0 m³
Annual fuel wood requirement/family	36.0 m³
Annual fuel wood requirement for communities	58.860 m³
Annual fuel wood requirement as a percentage of standing wood per hectare	22.8%
No. of years required to totally degrade a hectare by fuel wood harvesting and farming.	53 months or 4.4 years

Assuming an average farm size of 8 persons table 3 presents an analysis of the wood demands of the Tubah community. In 1998 the population dependent on the Tubah forest for their livelihood was estimated to be 18.891 inhabitants or 2362 farm families, with an estimated annual growth rate of 3.8%. This population will be 24.527 and 35.613 inhabitants in 2005 and 2015 respectively. Deforestation is attributed to slash-and-burn shifting cultivation, harvesting of construction wood and medicinal plants, fuel wood and inadequacies in the supply of forest products to the masses. The forest originally covered 3950 hectares. Today only 500 hectares of indigenous forest are left. Slash and burn shifting cultivation has degraded about 850 hectares and grazing by pastoral tribes an estimated 2509 hectares. The remaining indigenous forest is refuged in narrow upland riparian areas (Table 4).

Table 4: Vegetation and Land use on different sites (figure 2 and 3) for1950 and 2000

Land use and year	Forest area		Land use systems in 2000			Total forest
	1960	2000	Cultivation	Grazing	Fallow	
Bambili upland	750 ha (100%)	200ha (26%)	100 ha (13.3%)	250 ha (33.3%)	200 ha (26%)	550 ha (73.3%)
Bafunge Upland	1400 ha (100%)	240 ha (17.1%)	200 ha (14.2%)	959 ha (68.5%)	01 ha (0.07%)	1160 ha (82.8)
Tchabal Bamessing)	770 ha (100%)	60 ha (7.7%)	10 ha (0.1%)	600 ha (77.9%)	100 ha (12.9%)	720 ha (93.5%)
Bambili	600 ha (100%)	Totally Degraded (0.0%)	200 ha (33.3%)	400 ha (66.6%)	- (0.0%)	600 ha (100%)
Tchabal (Kedjom K)	430 ha (100%)	None left (0.0%)	250 ha (58.1%)	180 ha (41.8%)	- (0.0%)	430 ha (100%)
TOTAL	3950 ha	500 ha	760 ha	2509 ha	201 ha	3, 450 ha
Percentage	100	(12.6%)	(19.2)	(63.5%)	5.0%	87.3%

Table 4 presents the hectarage of the remaining forest, various land use systems that have replaced indigenous forest and the original forest cover in 1960 and 2000. Hawkins and Brunt. 1965, Nkwi and Warnier (1982), Tamura (1986), Kadomura (1984) and Letouzey (1968) report that the upland watersheds by 1960 had an almost unfragmented sub-montane forest cover. The first cattle rearers (Fulani tribe) settled in the Tehabal area in 1920 Nkwi and Warnier, 1982). About 250 farmers cultivate farm holdings in the forest riparian areas while the grazing of natural pastures on crests at elevations above 200^0 m has over the years resulted in the invasion of forests by

34

associated bush-fires and the browsing of shrubs by cattle. Grazing and slash-and-burn shifting cultivation have provoked a savannization of the area and a moribund vegetation landscape. Generally the derived natural pastures are in a poor state, badly eroded and have a very low fodder and a widespread growth of ferns (*Pteridium aquilinum*) between the dominating stubbles of *sporobolus* grass (Ndenecho, 2003).

Table 4 is derived from Figures 2 and 3. In 1960 the forest was still intact and had a surface area of 3950 hectares. Between 1960 and 2000 about 3, 450 hectares of forest were totally degraded (87.3%) by cultivation and fuel wood collection and grazing. Subsistence farming and associated bush fallows degraded 961 hectares of forest (24.3%) while grazing and associated bush fires 2509 hectares of forest (63.5%). Approximately a total of 86.3 hectares of forest were degraded per year between 1960 and 2000. Despite the national prohibition of uncontrolled fires, they continue to pose a threat to the remaining forest. In fire damaged areas, dead trees are being exploited for firewood. Many fire-damaged areas are used to cultivate beans, potatoes and cocoyams. Most of these fires are initiated by farmers, graziers, hunters and children. It must be noted that fuel wood extraction is not a major activity causing forest degradation. After areas have been cleared for farming then the remaining dead timber is removed for firewood. Similarly timber from areas of fire-damaged forest is utilized for fuel (Table 3). With the construction of the Bamenda-Fundong and Bamenda-Kumbo highway through Tubah in 1997 fuel wood extraction is increasing as it has become more profitable to sell. Growing urban populations are becoming more reliant on wood from rural areas, such as Tubah, to supply their needs. The effects of other livelihood activities such as extraction of bamboo, medicinal plants, collection of fruits, seeds and other forest products were not investigated.

Photo: Refugia of montane forest in the Tubah Mountain range (Bamenda Highlands)

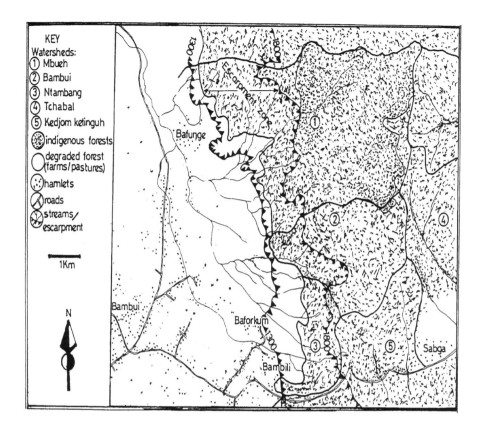

Figure 2: Tubah Upland Forest: Degradation situation as in 1960 Source: Compiled after Hawkins and Burnt (1965), (1986) Bawden and Langdale – Brown (1961) and 1967 IGN land use Map Nkambe-Wum

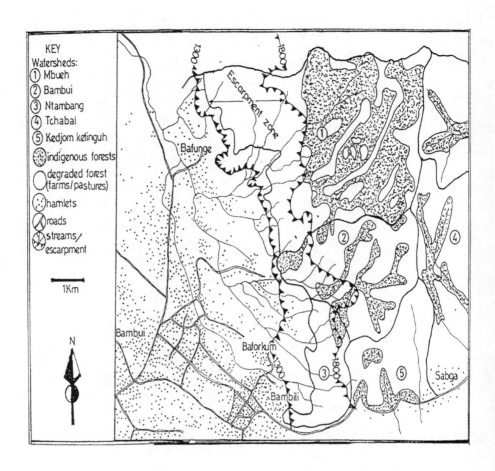

Figure 3: *Tubah Upland Forest: Degradation Situation as in 2000. Source: Ndenecho, 2003*

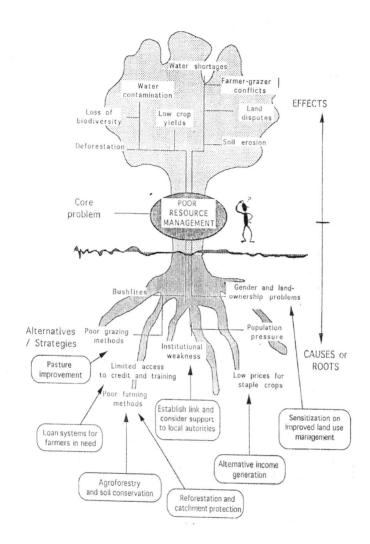

Figure 4: *Problem analysis of underlying causes of wood fuel shortages in Tubah Community (Zimmermann, 1996)*

Zimmermann (1996) identifies the underlying causes of the wood fuel shortages (figure 4). The core problem is unsustainable harvesting of products from forests and its side effects. The key issues involving fuel wood availability and food production are complex and inter-related (Poulsen, 1983; Chauvin, 1981; Ben Salem and Van Nao; 1981 and Beets, 1978). Working in Tubah upland watersheds Zimmermann (1996; 1994) identified the effects of the wood fuel crisis, their root causes and related issues. (Figure 4).

Apart from the fuel wood crisis, rural people sense the following effects of deforestation; loss of biodiversity, water contamination, soil erosion, dry season potable water shortages, farmer-grazier conflicts, land disputes and poor crop yields under slash-and-burn cultivation. These are the consequences of poor forest resources management whose root causes are: annual bush fires, grazing encroachment into forests, population pressure resulting in invasion of upland forests by landless farmers, institutional weakness and inefficient extension service, poor farming methods, poor grazing methods, and gender/land ownership problems related to adoption of agroforestry practices and the establishment of woodlots. Limited access to credit and training also hamper the adoption of agroforesty practices. The prices of staple foods are low hence obliging farmers to migrate to afro-alpine zones where market gardening is more profitable. Figure 4 identifies the strategies that can resolve the fuel wood scarcity problem using ecologically integrated land use systems.

Conclusion

These findings show that a more comprehensive and objective view of wood fuels is needed There are no single or simple answers and that the problems surrounding them are inseparably linked to the complex, diverse, extremely dynamic and multi-sectoral issues underlying the broader crisis of population pressure, food security, poverty, land and natural resource management. Successful remedies for the fuel wood crisis must therefore be firmly rooted in this broader context. Most farming systems in sub – Saharan Africa are subsistence systems where the use of land is directed towards satisfying the basic needs of food, fuel, fibre, medicine and shelter. It is therefore apparent that they constitute a prime area for the adoption of ecologically integrated land use systems and agroforestry must form an element of such systems. If interventions are to create lasting successes they must recognise at least three basic factors (Poulsen, 1983; Chauvin, 1981):

- The need for local assessment and actions and the unhelpful nature of large scale averages. The "landscapes" and "peoplescapes" of rural areas are extremely diverse. Problems and opportunities for solving them are therefore specific to place and social groups. The aim therefore should be to reach underlying causes rather than heal the symptoms;
- The need for indirect approaches to wood fuel issues and greater participation by local people at every stage to help them to prioritise and solve their own problems. This stems from the first point, and also from the fact that success normally depends on starting and strengthening processes

rather than delivering technical packages on "how" rather than "what" things are done; and

- The need for decentralized and multi-disciplinary approaches, including the use of competent and trusted "grassroots" agencies, to facilitate the two first points. However, this does not exclude the need for economic, legal and political initiatives at the macro-level to improve the broad contexts for local, positive change.

The study demonstrates that focusing development efforts on wood fuels and the symptoms of their scarcity is looking only at the tip of the proverbial iceberg. It ignores the much broader and deeper strains in the environmental, socio-economic and political fabric of which firewood scarcity is only one of the manifestations. These multi-faceted issues are diagnosed in chapter 2 using the Bafut-Ngemba Forest Reserve.

Acknowledgements

The study acknowledges the contribution of Kum Sylvester, Rolf Boiler and Yende Ernestine in the accomplishment of the forest survey.

References

Alpert, P. (1993) Conserving biodiversity in Cameroon. *Ambio* 22:44-49.

Bawden, M.G. and Langdale – Brown, I. (1961) An aerial photographic reconnaissance of the present and possible land use in the Bamenda area. Dept. of Technical Co-operation, D.O. S. Forestry and land use section. 25 p.

Beets, M.C. (1978) The agricultural environment of eastern and southern Africa and its use. *Agricultureal Environment* 4:5-4.

Ben Salem, B. and Van Nao, T. (1981) Fuel wood production in traditional farming systems. *Unasylva* 33 (131): 13-18.

Bowden, C. and Andrews, S (1994) Mount Kupe and its birds. *Bulletin African Bird Club* 1:13-16.

Chauvin, H. (1981) When an African city runs out of fuel. *Unasylva* 33 (133): 11-20.

Collar, N.J. and Stuart, S.N. (1988) Key forests for threatened birds in Africa. International Council for Bird Presentation, Cambridge. p. 11-16.

Dongmo, J-L (1984) Le role de Lhomme a traverse ses activités agricoles et pastorals dans l'evolution des milieux naturels sur les Hautes Terres de L'Ouest Cameroun. In: H. Kadomura (ed.) *Natural and man-induced environmental changes in tropical Africa*. Hokkaido University, Sapporo. p. 61 – 74

Dowsett, R.J. (1998) A preliminary natural history survey of Mambilla Plateau and some lowland forests of eastern Nigeria. Tauraco Research Report No. 1, Tauraco Press. 56 p.

Hawkins, P. and Brunt, M. (1965) Soils and ecology of west Cameroon. FAO Rome. 516 p.

Hoff, J.; Kips, P. and Awa (1987) Land evaluation: general methodology and results for the Ring Road. FAO/UNDP/IRA Ekona Soil Resources Project. Ekona. 516 p.

Kadomura, H. (1984) Problems of past and recent environmental changes in the humid areas of Cameroon. In: H. Kadomura (ed.) *Natural and man-induced environmental changes in tropical Africa*. Hokkaido University. Sapporo. p. 7-20.

Letouzey, R. (1968) Etude Phytogeograpique du Cameroun. Paul Chavalier, Paris 511 p.
Macleod, H. (1986) The conservation of Oku Mountain forest: Cameroon. ICBP Report, Cambridge. p. 64-65.

Morin, S. (19790 L'evolution recente et actuelle des milieux naturels au Cameroun central et occidental. *Communication presentée au Colloque SAPANRIT, Saint Dennis de la Reunion: 1979* 41 p.

Ndenecho, E. (20060 Sustaining mountain environments and rural livelihoods in Bamenda Highlands, Cameroon. Unique Printers, Bamenda. 184 p.

Ndenecho, E. (2003) A landscape ecological analysis of the Bamenda Highlands. Unpublished PhD Thesis, Department of Geography, University of Buea. 443 p.

Neba, A. (1999) Modern Geography of the Republic of Cameroon. Neba Publishers, Bamenda. p. 70-73.

Ngwa, J.A. (1979) A new Geography of Cameroon. Longman Group Limited, London. 151 p.

Nkwi, P.N. and Warnier, J – P (1982) Elements of a history of the Western Grassfields. Dept. of Sociology. University of Yaounde. 236 p.

Poulsen, G. (1983) Using farm trees for fuel wood. *Unasylva* 35 (141): 26-29.

Poschem, P. (1997) Forest and employment – Much more than meets the eye. *11th World Forestry Congress: 1977;* Antalya, Turkey. 15 p.

Soudan, J. and Zingari, p. (2000) Mountain forest and employment in Savoy, France. Mountain Research and Development 20 (1): 132: 35.

Stuart, S.N. (1986) Conservation of Cameroon Montane forest. ICBP. Cambridge p. 6-11.

Tamura, T. (1986) Regolith-Stratigraphic Study of Late-Quaternary environmental history in the West Cameroon Highlands and the Adamaoua Plateau. In: H. Kadomura (ed.) *Geomorphology and environmental changes in Tropical Africa: Case studies in Cameroon and Kenya.* University of Hokkaido, Sapporo. p. 63-93.

Thomas, D. and Thomas, J. (1996) Tchabal Mbabo Botanical Survey. Consultants' Report to WWF Programme Office 44 p.

Zimmermann, T. (1994) Introduction to watershed management for intake areas of rural water supplies in Cameroon. In: *Proceedings of Agro-forestry Harmonisation Workshop: 4th – 7th April, 1994.* RCA Bambili. p. 20-27.

Zimmermann, T. (1996) Land use management and conservation farming practices. Helvetas-Cameroon, Bamenda. 96 p.

44

Chapter 3

Population Dynamics, Livelihoods and Forest Protection

Case study: Bafut-Ngemba Forest Reserve

Summary

The study makes a critical examination of mainstream efforts to rehabilitate and conserve forests in Cameroon and concludes that technocratic blue-prints will always founder when they come face-to-face with the real world of complex human relation in poverty stricken societies. These result from the failure to integrate the concerns relating to rights, needs and priorities of rural communities who are the local natural resource users. The chapter argues that when rural livelihoods are affected negatively the forest adjacent communities often respond in ways involving conflict, illegal exploitation of resources, and apathy which makes the realisation of conservation goals very remote. There is therefore a need for a broader perspective that links environmental protection with human welfare. Consequently, the study advocates that Social Impact Assessment (SIAs) be an integral part of such conservation projects if successes have to be registered.

Key Words: Population dynamics, Livelihoods, Forest protection, human welfare, social impact assessment.

Introduction

Over the past two or three decades there has been a seemingly positive aspect of development process and strategies in most of Sub- Saharan Africa, that is, the upsurge in environmental protection schemes. The goal has been to conserve and rehabilitate ecosystems, forest, and soil and water resources. Utting (1994) observes that the concrete experience of policy, programme and project implementation in the field of environmental protection has raised serious doubts over the capacity of such schemes to contribute to sustainable development in general and human welfare in particular. He emphasized the fact that the design and implementation of policies, programmes and projects have been concerned essentially with trying to minimize the trade-off between economic growth and social marginalisation and environmental degradation affecting both present and future generations. Measures coined to protect or rehabilitate ecosystems often impinge negatively on livelihoods at the village level or involve benefits which accrue mainly to local elites (Ndenecho, 2005). Cameroon has established about 43 forest reserves (MINEF/ ONADEF, 1993), which do not more than protect ravaged, degraded sites. But forest reserves that ignore their human neighbours and that cannot stave off the insidious encroachment of millions of small farmers and fuelwood gatherers, many of whom live in absolute poverty. These are doomed to fail.

There has been a tendency to analyse the failure of these projects largely in terms of technical, administrative, and financial constraints or the limited environmental commitment or awareness of policy makers and natural resource users (Besong and Ngwasiri, 1995; Utting, 1994). The central argument of this paper is that most environmental protection projects have failed as a result of micro-incoherencies, that is, the failure to integrate the concerns for environmental protection with those relating to the rights, needs and priorities of local communities who are the local natural resource users. When livelihoods are affected negatively the forest adjacent communities often respond in ways involving conflict, illegal exploitation of resources and apathy which makes the realisation of projects goals remote. There is therefore a need for a broader perspective that links environmental protection with human welfare.

Santa is an administrative district in the Bamenda Highlands of Cameroon. The dominant geographical feature is a high lava plateau dominated by Mount Lefo (2550 metres). Most the plateau is above 1500m and 2000m altitude with a cool and misty climate. Average annual maximum temperature ranges between 20.5°C and 23.3°C while the minimum is between 12.6°C and 14.2°C. A dry season occurs from mid-November to mid- March and the average annual rainfall is about 2286 mm. The soils are humic ferrallitic soils developed on humic lava. There are mountain forest refugia in remote escarpment zones and on high mountain peaks. The cloudy and misty climate is reflected by the profusion of mosses, lichens, epiphytic and orchids which festoon the trees. Trees include *Albezia, Allophilus, Nuxia congesta, Polyscia fulva, Pygeum africanus, Syzgium spp. Scheffler spp. Bridelia m., Maesa lonceolata, Trema guineensis, Rapanea neurophylla, Aguara solicifolia, Hypericum revolutum, Lasiosiphon glaucus and Murica arborea.* The forests are cut over for timber and firewood in an unsystematic way. Slash and burn farming, grazing encroachment and bush fires have ravaged the forest. Illegal poaching is common. Abundant resources for ethno-medicine are being tapped. The threatened potentials and assets include: medicinal plants, rare and endemic bird life and monkeys, diverse and endemic vascular plants. Two forest reserves represent the remnants of these forests. These are the Bafut-

Ngemba Forest Reserve and the Bali-Ngemba Forest Reserve. The remaining native forests in the reserve have been described by Ndikefor (2003).

A good number of species in the indigenous forest are of important conservation concern. The secondary forest is made up of patches of pure and mixed woods of eucalyptus, cypress and pine most of them at the stage of exploitation. Presently, it constitutes about 70% of the remaining forest. There is still a lot of bird life and some mammals, some of which are near extinction. Birds such as various Turacos and related species are frequently seen. Also found in the forest patches are a small population of monkeys, gazelles, snakes and rare and endemic frogs and birds in the lake. These features suggest that the forest was once continuous with other montane forests of the Bamenda Highlands. Rich melliferous plants support two bee species and apiculture in and at the forest margin is an important livelihood activity.

The area has a very important diversity of plants and animals and considerable water resources. Amongst the plant resources are special forest resources like *Prunus africana* (medicinal) which is exploited for its bark, as well as some plants of conservation concern like *Arundinaria alpina* (Alpine bamboo), found again only in Kilum/Ijim and Bambotous in the whole of Cameroon., *Lobelia columnalis* and some edible tree mushrooms. The animal resources need urgent attention: the Black Monkey which is an endangered animal, so far recorded in Mount Cameroon, Mount Oku and Obudu plateau in Nigeria. Other mammals like the giant rats, marsh cane rats, squirrels, bay, dickers and serials are also found. Forest and lake frogs are seriously endangered by deforestation. The important bird species of conservation concern so far identified in this area are: Banded-wattle eye *(Platysteria laticincta)*, Bannerman's weaver *((Ploceus bannermani)*, Bannman's Turaco *(Turaco Bannermani)*, Bangwa forest warbler *(Bradypsterus bangwaensis)*, Cameroon montane greenbul *(Andropedus Montanus)* (Macleod, 1986).

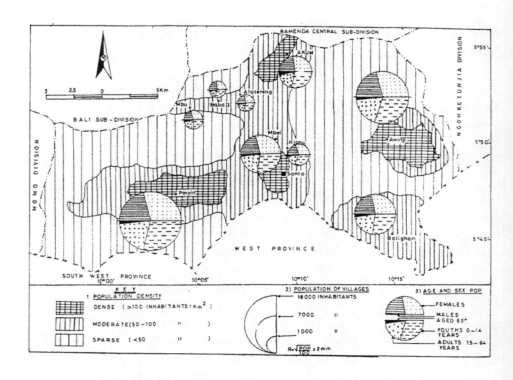

Figure 1: Density, Age and Sex Distribution of population in Santa

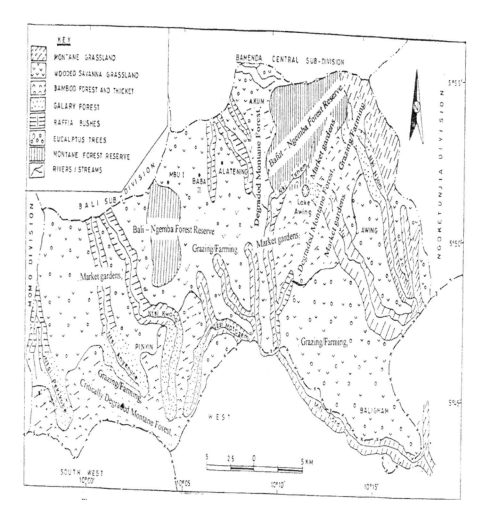

Figure 2: Savanization Process and Remnants of Montane Forests and Gallery forests of Raffia palms in Santa

Table 1:   The spatial distribution of population in Santa (see Figure 1)

Village	Population	% of total population	Male No.	%	Female No.	%
Akum	4.487	7.8	1.999	44.6	2.488	55.4
Alatening	1.226	2.13	552	45	674	55.0
Awing	14.570	25.3	6.838	46.9	7.732	53.1
Baba II	1.213	2.1	570	47	643	53.0
Baligham	7.344	18.8	3.372	45.9	3.972	54.1
Mbei	6.071	10.6	2.753	45.4	3.314	54.6
Mbu	1.985	3.5	944	47.6	1.041	52.4
Njong	1.676	2.9	794	47.4	882	52.6
Pinyin	18.887	32.9	8.843	46.8	10.044	53.2
Total	**57.759**	**100**	**26.669**		**30.790**	

Source: Provincial Service of Statistics and National Accounting, Bamenda, 1997.

Table 1 presents the population of nine village communities that constitute Santa district. The average population density is approximately 178 inhabitants per square kilometre but there are however pockets of very high population density above 200 inhabitants/km^2. There is certainly pressure on available cultivable land. The humic ferrallitic soils and the climate favour market-oriented gardening, the cultivation of Irish potatoes and maize. The slash-and-burn shifting cultivation degraded the montane forests to savanna or grassfields. The typical succession after forest clearance has been described by Hawkins and Brunt (1965):

- **1st year:** Rank weed growth dominated by members of the *compositaceae, Erigeron floribundus* dorminates together with *Ageratium conyzoides, Anisopapus africanus, Bidens pilosa, Conyza aegytica, Guizota scabra, Laggera alata and Laggera pterodonta.* The annual grass *Rhnchelytrum repens* is often also abundant on first year fallows.
- **2nd Year:** Invasion by the *Imperata Cyclindrica* (Spear grass), which may become dominant towards the end of the wet season or growing season.
- **3rd Year:** Invasion by the grasses *Hyparrahenia, Digitaria spp.* and *Melinus minutiflora* (Molasses grass).
- **4th and 5th Years:** Fourth and fifth year fallows are rare. However, in the less densely populated areas these can be identified. Observations showed a gradual decline in the dominance of *Imperata cyclindrica* and in *Hyparrhenia* dominance.

The farmers rely upon the successions described above to build up the organic matter in the soil, and thereby to partially restore its depleted nutrient status. Such a fallow system is satisfactory when there is plenty of land to spare. Due to high population growth rates, areas of denser population have shorter duration fallows. Farmers are obliged to migrate and invade upland watersheds, montane forest reserves and to encroach into afro-alpine grasslands. The tendency towards reduced fallows and permanent farming systems with short fallow durations results in the degradation of the climatic climax vegetation and a savannisation process. To meet the high demand for food, these villages are now facing difficulties in adapting to rapid demographic growth, increasing market orientation of agricultural production, the ongoing economic depression with unattractive prices for agricultural products and ecological marginalisation. The farming techniques developed over centuries are no longer able to sustain the fragile balance between production and conservation. The only way out has been to extend farm boundaries into forest reserves (hollow frontiers), upland watersheds and afro-alpine natural pastures. Farm sizes have been shrinking. According to the Santa Sub-Divisional Delegation for Agriculture, the average farm size lies between 0.5 to 0.8 hectares for an average farm family size of eight.

The landscape is a mosaic of grassfields, fallow plots, gallery forest patches and natural pastures. The grazing system can be described as an extensive system with transhumance and the plateau constitute the wet season pastures while the valleys and lake basin constitute dry season grazing sites. There is equally the invasion of forest reserves by cattle during the dry season (See figure 2). The destruction of riparian and montane vegetation has led to a decline in nesting places for many rare and endemic montane birds. Many rare mammals are threatened with habitat loss. Due to this invasion, young trees are browsed when soft and succulent and eventually die off causing widespread loss of nesting and roosting habitats for birds and other animals that use the mountain forests. Population pressure and the search for livelihood activities is imposing biological stresses on the forest reserves. The 1987 population of Santa was 57,459 inhabitants according to the National Population and Housing Census. With a growth rate of 2.04% per annum, it is estimated to be 82,622 and 101,095 inhabitants by 2005 and 2015 respectively. In 1987, the average population density was 142 inhabitants/km^2. This rose to 178 inhabitants per km^2 in 1998. The data presented above highlights the need for a more integrative and socially aware approach to environmental planning and project design and implementation so that projects do not negatively impinge on the livelihoods of the landless and disadvantaged members of the villages. The main threats to the reserves are (Chefor, 2002). See Figure 3.

o   All year round market gardening;
o   Harvesting of non-timber forest products;
o   Harvesting of timber and fuel wood;
o   Food crop farming under slash-and-burn shifting cultivation system and the clear-bury-and-burn system;
o   Extensive grazing of alpine grasslands and forest undergrowth;
o   Hunting and trapping of animals; and
o   Establishment of squatter settlements by migrant graziers/farmers.

These threats cast doubts over the capacity of the mountain forest conservation projects to contribute to sustainable development in general and human welfare in particular. Apart from ensuring that the fundamental objectives of the projects are achieved, do these projects address the rights and needs of more marginal groups in the village communities? The forest reserves were created in the 1940s in view of the importance of their biodiversity, scientific and tourist interests during the British Colonial period in the country. After independence in 1960, experiences show that forest protection by itself does not work. The problem is often reduced to inadequate size of budgets and foreign aid by the National Forest Development Authority (NFDA) and non-governmental organisation concerned with conservation of the forests. The NFDA also points to the limitations on the quantity and quality of human resources, for example, forest guards to police and administer protected areas and forestry technicians to provide extension services. Putting artificial fences around forests and calling them reserves is almost certain to fail because people are hungry. The forest adjacent communities live in poverty. Hungry resource and poor people cannot ignore livelihoods that can be made from montane forests. The important question is how to find ways of using the forests without destroying them. There is need for a link between human welfare, environmental protection and sustainable natural resource usage.

Research Methods

The study used the 1987 National Population and Housing Census results and base maps to generate data on population dynamics. Base maps and aerial photographs were used to complement field observations in establishing the extent of human encroachment in the Bafut-Ngemba Forest Reserve. Three forest adjacent village communities around this reserve were selected for study. These were Akum, Awing and Njong-Bamock. Data on land pressure and conflicts was obtained from documented sources. Using the local Agricultural posts for each village data on the farming population and forest dependent population was obtained. The data so obtained was used together with open questions to assess the farmers' awareness to the status of the montane forest as a protected area and their perception of the conservation project. Informal interviews with the NGO operating in forest rehabilitation (Greenlife International) and local National Forest Development Authority (NFDA) yielded data on the various threats to the forest conservation schemes of the highlands as a whole.

Presentation of Results and Discussions

Figure 3 presents a cross-section through the Bafut-Ngemba Forest Reserve. It highlights the main anthropogenic threats to the reserve which are summarized here. Food and cash crop farming have fragmented several parts of the reserve. The profitability of vegetable and potato farming in these afro-alpine conditions has risen dramatically in the last 10 years. Migrant farmers' squatters are littered in most remote parts of the reserve. Livestock form an important part of the local economy and together with the pressure on land have engendered several conflicts.

Table 2: Land use conflicts recorded between 1995 and 2004 in Santa

Months	Farmer-Grazier conflicts		Farmer-Farmer conflicts	
	No.	Percentage	No.	Percentage
January	16	10.7	12	6.9
February	12	08.0	14	8.0
March	18	12.0	18	10.3
April	10	06.7	16	9.1
May	15	10.0	14	8.0
June	09	06.0	14	8.0
July	05	03.3	15	8.6
August	05	03.0	18	10.3
September	10	06.7	15	8.6
October	17	11.3	13	7.4
November	15	10.0	10	5.7
December	18	12.0	16	9.1
Total	150	100	175	100

Source: Pinyin Interim Clan Council (P.I.C.C), with modifications.

Table 2 presents the various land use conflicts in Santa. These occur on fields in both riparian areas and montane areas where the interests of farmers and graziers conflict. All grazing and farming within the reserve is prohibited but illegal farming and grazing is common and sheep, goats and cattle range freely in parts of the reserve. Migrant farmers and graziers use fire to degrade portions of the forest before farming and grazing respectively. Bush fires also emanate from the harvesting of wild honey and charcoal burners who operate in parts of the reserve. Trees have to be killed and logged for fuelwood. Medicinal plants such as the *Prenus africanus* are extracted from the forest. This is a tree of the Rosaceae family. Its bark produces a drug which helps control urinary complaints resulting from enlarged prostate glands. Illegal and unsustainable exploitation has killed several trees. Hunting used to be an important occupation and the forests were occasionally burnt to flush out small mammals, which were caught. Most large mammals have been hunted out, though there are still populations of bushbuck and monkey. The land use conflicts presented in table 2 certainly reflect the "tragedy of the commons" in the use of a resource in a society.

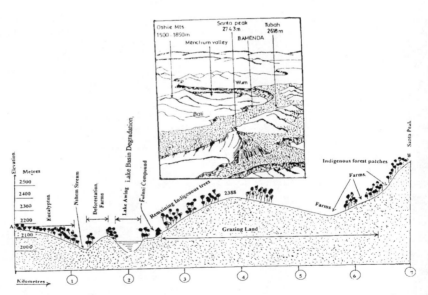

Figure 3: Block diagram showing Santa Peak – Tubah Mountain range and cross section through Santa (Mount Lefo forest): Fragmented montane forest.

Table 3: Reported cases of crop damage by free ranging cattle in Santa.

Year	No. of registered cases	Crops damage	Total area destroyed (hectares)
1995 - 1996	25	Cabbage, maize, Leeks, beans, Irish potato	15
1996 - 1997	14	Maize, beans potato	12
1997 - 1998	17	Potato, maize, beans, leeks, sweat potato	10
1998 – 1999	23	Carrots, potato, cabbage, leeks, potato	13
1999 – 2000	10	Maize, beans, cabbage, leeks, potato	09
Total	**89**	**All crops**	**59**

Source: Santa Rural Council, 2002

Table 3 reveals that between 1995 and 2004 the district recorded 150 farmer-grazier conflicts and 175 farmers – farmer conflicts over land us rights. This gives an average of 36 conflicts per year. Such conflicts certainly give momentum to the ecological marginalisation of weaker members of the society and contribute to increasing impoverishment and /or inequality of local people. Table 3 shows the extent of crop damages involved in such conflicts. On the average about 11.9 hectares of market gardens are damaged annually by the invasion of gardens by cattle. The responses of local people to the land use pressure and to the need for access to safe access to key production resources is to further encroach on the reserve borders and remote riparian valleys within the reserve. These undermine the possibility of effectively implementing forest protection measures. It is therefore crucial for protection projects to focus more on the trade-off between forest protection and the human welfare of the forest adjacent communities, that is, addressing the rights and needs of more marginal groups in society as well as ensuring that fundamental conservation objectives are achieved in practice (Denniston, 1995).

Table 4: Age Distinction of Farming population depending on the forest (forest adjacent villages)

Village Community	Male N°.	Female N°.	Total N°.	<15 Years		16 – 25 Years		26 – 35 Years		35+ Year	
				N°.	%	N°.	%	N°.	%	N°.	%
Awing	250	800	1050	132	12.5	263	19.3	525	50.0	130	12.3
Akum	150	300	450	60	13.3	113	25.1	225	50.0	52	11.5
Njong / Bamock	47	142	189	26	13.3	47	8.9	95	50.0	22	11.6

The study identified the more marginal groups in the three forest adjacent village communities. These are presented in table 4. The table presents the age distribution of villagers illegally farming in the forest reserve. Youths between 15 and 35 years account for 69.3% of farmers from Awing village, 75.1% of farmers from Akum and 59.1% of farmers from Njong-Bamock. Those above 35 years of age constitute about 12% of the farmers. These youths are responding to increasing pressures on available land resources, increasing rural unemployment, increasing market- orientation of farming and other livelihood activities. Most of them are squatters who specialize in crops with very short vegetative cycles such as vegetables and Irish potatoes. Children below 15 years account for about 13% of those farming in the forest. Child labour is hired for irrigation, spraying of vegetables with agro-chemicals, nursery management and transportation of produce.

Table 5: Population with forest dependent livelihoods in Santa

Village	Population	Farming Population		Forest dependent Population	
		Population	Percentage	Population	Percentage of Farmers
Awing	14570	12238	83.9	1050	8.5
Akum	4487	3813	84.9	450	11.8
Njong	1676	1525	90.0	189	12.3

The forest adjacent communities are mainly involved in agriculture as a livelihood activity. Only about six families are involved in livestock raising. They live in two clusters and maintain some 1500 cattle, 200 sheep and 100 horses. From table 5 approximately 80 to 90% of the population are farmers and 8 to 12% of the farming population derives a livelihood by the exploitation of the forest reserve. Within the traditional land tenure system by either inheritance or the lease system access to land as a key production asset to young people aspiring to be farmers is very difficult given that most of the land within homesteads is under coffee plantations and tended by old people. Market gardening is a relatively new farming activity involving mainly young people or school leavers who are landless or marginalized by the traditional land tenure system. They are therefore obliged to fetch for land in marginal ecological zones. This study refers to this socially disadvantaged group as "migrant farmers". The success of any conservation project depends on their recognition, adequate planning procedures which adopt long-term horizons, which consult with local people and which convince local natural resource users of the need to adapt their practices to project goals. The NFDA and NGOs operating in the area have introduced schemes to promote reforestation of the fragmented portions of the reserves. The seedlings are provided to farmers for integration in the areas critically degraded by farming as a concession to the migrant farmers who in turn must manage the trees planted. This has not yielded any good results. Increasingly, the crucial question of how to integrate these migrant farmers and local communities in the forest protection schemes is being posed by NFDA, and a number of NGOs are encouraging this approach.

Table 6: Farmers responses to the awareness of who owns the forest reserve

Awareness as a percentage of population							
Village community	Farming population depending on the forest	State owned forest: protected (reserve)		Open access resource for the village (adjacent communities)		Do not know who owns the forest		Observation
	(No.)	No.	%	No.	%	No.	%	
Awing	1050	600	57	325	30.9	124	11.8	There is still great need for the state to educate local people on forest resource ownership and management
Akum	450	202	44.8	98	21.7	150	33.3	
Njong/ Bamock	189	125	66.1	04	2.1	60	31.7	

People from forest adjacent communities complain of being harassed by forest guards when in their quest for livelihood activities in the forest. They cannot understand how their indigenous and local forests became state forests. Table 4 presents the awareness of local people to the question of ownership of the forest. Approximately 35 to 40% of the farming population in the forest from adjacent communities does not regard the state as owner of the forest. This certainly makes implementation of the project extremely difficult. The consequence of these livelihood activities has been the extensive degradation of the semi-humid evergreen montane forest. It has in most areas been completely cut down by migrant farmers from adjacent villages and reduced to marginal farmlands, fallows and grazing lands. Bush fires have reduced the secondary forest of eucalyptus, pine and cypress and illegal exploitation to scattered stands and clumps. In short, the state of degradation on about 3000 hectares of the reserve can be described as critical despite on-going rehabilitation and conservation programmes.

Table 7: Percentage farmers willing to cooperate with the conservationservice

Village community	Farming population depending on the forest (No.)	Willing to respect laws/ regulations		Not willing to respect laws/ regulations		Neutral farmers	
		No.	%	No.	%	No.	%
Awing	1050	725	69	200	19	175	12
Akum	450	352	78.2	76	16.8	22	4.8
Njong/ Bamock	189	185	97.8	03	1.6	01	0.5

Observation: *A good proportion of local people are willing to cooperate with the state to manage forest resources but the conviction still needs to be created through education sensitisation, and dialogue.*

Table 7 presents the responses of farmers operating in the forest when asked about their willingness to support the conservation and rehabilitation projects. About 20 to 30% of the farmers are not readily willing to cooperate with the project administration, as they are not stakeholders. This project was set up without their involvement and is drastically restricting their access to key resources for survival. Since these farmers have no alternative income generating activities, they are hostile to the reserve. Approximately 69 to 80% are willing to cooperate with the project hoping that it will offer and guarantee alternative resources for a livelihood. While it is apparent that the environmental conservation drive has gathered momentum in recent years, there is still a wide gap between government rhetoric and policy objectives, on the one hand, and the reality of policy and project implementation on the other (Utting, 1994). Numerous regulations and laws remain unenforced, projects poorly implemented, while measures to protect or rehabilitate the forest impinge on the local people's livelihoods. NFDA and the Ministry of Forests and Environment responsible for encouraging tree planting and protection of the reserve are fairly weak. These protection projects apart from ignoring the pressing need of the rural poor for basic food supplies, also ignore the complex and heterogeneous nature of the livelihood system of land users. Many policies and schemes give insufficient attention to the socio-economic and cultural situation of local populations whose livelihoods depend on resources found in such areas. Attempts by the NFDA and NGOs to rehabilitate the forest are often contradicted by other "development" measures by the departments of Agriculture and Animal Husbandry which degrade the forests.

Conclusions

Conservation projects in the Bamenda Highlands are still characterised by a narrow sectoral focus. Attention has not been paid to the broader development context and the linkages of poverty, capital accumulation and environmental degradation. The Ministries of Agriculture and Livestock respond to different pressure groups and ideologies which apart from these ages old conflicts in the region also tend to generate certain types of social responses and conflicts which undermine forest conservation efforts. The top-down approach has also tended to characterise the design and implementation of these conservation schemes. There is no appropriate framework instituted by NFDA for inter-agency co-ordination, involvement of the Santa Municipal Authority and Local NGOs. There is an urgent need to consider the linkages in the region, between the process of forest destruction on one hand, and the crisis of subsistence procurement and the lack of alternative employment and income generating opportunities on the other. Until projects sufficiently address this issue, forest conservation projects will hardly attain their goals in sub-Saharan Africa. There will also be a need to tackle problems of land tenure and access to land as a key production resource. The use of forest reserves as the "commons" has been a factor underpinning deforestation. Attention has been focused exclusively on the protected forests and the social, economic, cultural and land tenure situation of people in forest adjacent areas disregarded. The forest reserves have not been integrated with the local inhabitants. Integration requires intensive dialogue with various local groups in the design stage of forest protection and tree planting projects. Social Impact Assessments (SIAs) need to be an integral part of such projects and should:

- identify the groups that stand to gain or lose from the protection project;
- identify potential conflicts of interest and elaborate conflict resolution mechanisms;
- consider the responses of the forest adjacent communities as well as the social and environmental implications of such responses when their livelihoods and interests are negatively affected; and
- explore and develop alternative livelihood scenarios for individuals and groups negatively affected by the conservation project.

The above considerations are necessary to address the rights and needs of more marginal groups and also to ensure that fundamental conservation objectives can be achieved in practice. Only in this way can most conservation projects in Sub-Saharan Africa free themselves from the bitter experience that technocratic blue-prints founders when they stand face to face with the real world of complex human relations in poverty stricken communities. Chapter 4 emphasizes the complex problems mitigating against sustainable forest protection.

References

Besong, J. and Ngwasiri, C. (1995): *The 1994 forestry law and national forest resource management in Cameroon.* PVO – NGO/NRMS Cameroon Publication.

Chefor, E. (2002): *Project proposal: Awing watershed rehabilitation and conservation.* Greenlife Foundation International, Bamenda.

Denniston, D. (1995): *Sustaining mountain peoples and environments.* In: World Watch Institute Report of Progress towards sustainable society, titled: State of the world, 1995. W. W. Norton and Company, New York.

Hawkins, P. and Brunt. M. (1965): *Soils and ecology of West Cameroon.* Report No. 2083, FAO Rome.

Macleod, H. (1986): *The conservation of Oku Mountain forest, Cameroon.* Study Report No. 15. International Council for Bird Preservation, Cambridge.

MINEF/ONADEF (1993): *Cameroon's forests: for a sustainable and lasting management.* National Forest Development Agency, Yaounde.

Ndenecho, E. (2005): *Biological resource exploitation in Cameroon: from crisis to sustainable management.* Unique Printers, Bamenda.

Ndikefor, T. (2003): *Conservation of the Bafut-Ngemba forest.* Industrial Attachment Report, Regional College of Agriculture, Bambili, Bamenda.

Utting, P. (1994): *Social and Political Dimensions of Environmental Protection in Central America.* In: G. Dharam (ed.) Development and environment: sustaining people and nature. Blackwell Publishers/UNRISD.

62

Chapter 4

Livelihoods and Threats to Biodiversity Management

Case study: Mount Cameroon Project

Summary

The problems facing the sustainable conservation and management of biodiversity in Sub-Saharan Africa have tended to be defined in ways that do not lead to acceptable solutions. The chapter uses a combination of primary and secondary data sources to identify the problems mitigating against a sustainable biodiversity management in Sub-Saharan Africa. It posits that both the problems and the solutions are built on economic foundations that need to be clearly understood. The most costly and least effective management strategy is to rely on state power. Most of the forest with protection status exists only on paper. The chapter concludes that failure results from the fact that the rights which are denied forest-adjacent villages are so basic to livelihoods that enforcement is ineffective and imposes considerable social costs. Ill adapted strategies that undermine rural livelihoods are bound to fail. Identifying the complex problems mitigating against sustainable management, the chapter argues for elaborate new models for wildlife management. It recommends a holistic wildlife management model which simultaneously addresses the pillars of sustainability (economic, productive, environmental, social and cultural) using the community forestry approach.

Introduction

Today's threat to species and ecosystems is the greatest recorded in history (McNeely *et al*; 1990). Virtually all of them are caused by human mismanagement of biological resources, often stimulated by misguided economic policies and faulty institutions that enable the exploiters to avoid paying the full costs of their exploitation. Solutions to the problem of biodiversity degradation depend above all on how the problem is defined. It appears that the problems facing the conservation of biological diversity in Sub-Saharan Africa have tended to be defined in ways that do not lead to acceptable solutions. The problems are generally defined in terms of insufficient areas, excess poaching (Jaff, 1994), poor law enforcement, land encroachment and illegal trade (Ndenecho, 2005; Denniston, 1995, Balgah, 2001).

These definitions warrant possible responses which include establishing more protected areas, improving standards of managing species and protected areas, enacting national forest protection laws, enacting international legislation controlling trade in endangered species and policing of protected areas. These measures are all necessary but they respond to only part of the problem. Fundamental problems lie beyond protected areas which affect the livelihoods of those who mismanage the natural resource base. This chapter seeks to identify the problems mitigating against biodiversity management by appraising the current management strategies and to identify alternative strategies for Sub-Saharan Africa.

The study area is located between latitudes 4^0N and 6^0 50'N and longitudes 8^0 50'E and 10^0E. It covers a surface area of 24,910km^2 (Figure 1). Geographically, this ecoregion encompasses the mountains and highland areas of the border between Nigeria and Cameroon excluding the Bamenda Highlands. It covers the Rumpi Hills, the Bakossi Mountains, Mount Nlonako, Mount Kupe and Mount Manenguba. (Stuart 1986; Gartland, 1989; Scatterfield *et al.*, 1998). Mount Cameroon is the dominant geographical feature with an altitude of 4100m. Most of the region is below 2000m in elevation. At about 800m to 1000m the ecoregion grades into lowland vegetation communities of other ecoregions. In the majority of cases, however, the lower boundary of these forests is now determined by conversion to agricultural land.

Rainfall is around 4000mm per annum, declining inland to 1800mm or less. The mean, temperatures are below 20^0C due to the effects of altitude. This is a volcanic region. Soils derived from volcanoes are fertile, which makes the land attractive to farmers. Combined with adequate rainfall, this contributes to a high human population density.

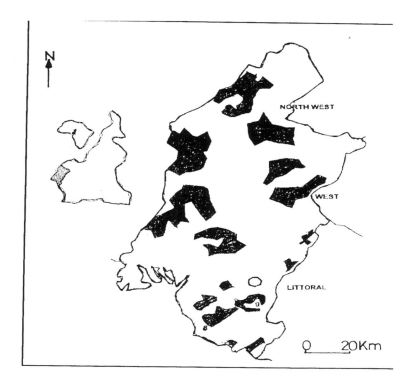

Figure 1: Location of the study area and the protected areas of South Western Cameroon.

In White's (1983) phytogeographical classification, these mountain areas fall within the Afromontane ecoregion. It has several endemic vascular plants and reptiles. Nine of the reptiles are considered narrow endemics (Stuart 1986). In addition to the narrow endemics, there is also a significant overlap between the flora and fauna of the mountains of this ecoregion. There are 50 endemic plant species and 30 near endemic plant species (White, 1983).

Human activities are increasingly fragmenting, degrading and isolating the remaining forest patches. The Bakossi Mountains have at least 200km^2 of mid-altitude and montane forest above the altitude of 1000m; and the lowland forest (Western Bakossi) covers some 400km^2. The study concentrated on the Western Bakossi forest: Banyang – Mbo forest reserves (42.606 hectares) created in 1936, Bambuko Forest Reserve (26,677 hectares) created in 1950, Southern Bakundo Forest Reserve (19,425 hectares) created in 1940, Mokoko River Forest Reserve (9,065 hectares) created in 1952, Bakossi Forest Reserve (5,517 hectares) created in 1956, Meme River Reserve (5,80 hectares) created in 1951 and Barombi – Mbo River Reserve created in

1950 (Asong, 2001). This is one of the least well protected eco-regions in Africa where local traditional rulers still exert considerable authority over land use. The main section of Bakossi (550km^2) became a "protection forest", banning all logging in 2000. Kupe became a "strict nature reserve". The boundaries were delimited by the participation of local people in 2000 – 2001.

The main objective is to ensure sustainable resource management with emphasis on natural regeneration, the involvement of the local population and the promotion of sustainable livelihoods by implementing the 1995 wildlife management laws and guidelines (Fonyam, 2001). The law recognizes the creation of buffer zones around all protected areas. These are regions adjacent to protected areas, which provide local communities with sustainable income generating activities (hunting, selective logging, fuel wood and non-timber forest products) (Jongman, 1995; Kelkit *el al*; 2005):

- Zone 1: a natural zone where nature has priority of protection
- Zone 2: a cultural zone sustaining local peoples livelihoods
- Zone 3: an intense usage zone with many land use systems
- Zone 4: a rehabilitation zone with emphasis on restoration of biodiversity and natural landscapes.

Research Methods

The study used a combination of primary and secondary sources to investigate the micro-incoherencies and constraints to biodiversity management. The conservation efforts of wildlife management workers were assessed by administering a questionnaire to 49 workers. This questionnaire focused on the main wildlife conservation activities and how they relate to the management strategy of the protected areas. Local communities adjacent to the protected areas with forest-dependent livelihoods were also investigated. Due to the large size of the study area, it was divided into five zones to ease data collection. These zones were:

- Zone A: villages in Mbonge area
- Zone B: villages in Munyenge in Muyuka
- Zone C: villages in Nguti and Bangem
- Zone D: villages in Bayang and Manyu
- Zone E: villages in Kupe Manenguba

240 questionnaires were administered in each zone to forest-adjacent residents. A total of 1200 questionnaires were administered. The questionnaires focused on the identification of livelihood activities,

quantitative and qualitative assessment of livelihood activities, forest users per protected area and buffer zone and forest exploitation techniques. Field visits involved the use of Participatory Rural Appraisal, and semi-structured interviews to obtain information on user groups of the forest. These tools were also used to identify the human activities and impacts on the forest. Aerial photographs were used to complement qualitative data on land use impacts on the Kupe forest, and the South Bakundu Forest Reserve. The study was complemented by secondary data and field observations. Of the 1200 copies of questionnaires distributed to the local population, a total of 934 were returned (77.8%).

- 1140 questionnaires were distributed to the local population and 885 were returned (77.6%), and
- 60 questionnaires were distributed to wildlife conservation technicians and 49 were returned (81.7%).

Rural livelihoods dependent on the protected areas were investigated using a combination of field observations of the Mount Kupe and South Bakundu areas. Land use maps from these field sites were facilitated by the work of Effange (2006), Ewane (2006) and Mesumbe (2001). These were updated using a Global Positioning System (GPS). Data on livelihoods dependent on the protected areas were obtained from secondary sources (Ewane, 2006; Effange, 2006) and the medicinal plant collection of the Limbe Botanic Garde which is yet to be published. The data so obtained was analysed using descriptive statistical techniques such as tables, frequencies and percentages in order to establish the constraints and micro-incoherencies in biodiversity management in traditional societies.

Presentation of Results And Discussions

Table 1: Main activities of wildlife conservation workers in Bamboko Forest Reserve and Bayang – Mbo wildlife sanctuary.

Main activities		Frequency	Percentage
1	Policing and guarding of protected area	28	57.1
2	Routine boundary demarcation/clearing	04	8.2
3	Research and Species identification	09	18.4
4	Regeneration/rehabilitation of degraded	06	12.2
5	areas	02	4.1
	No job specifications		
Total		49	100

Source: 2006 Fieldwork

Table 1 presents the main activities of the forest conservation workers. Their main function is routine policing and guarding of the protected areas (57.1%). There is little research on species identification which engages only 18.4% of the workers. Routine boundary demarcation and regeneration /rehabilitation of degraded area suffer from acute shortage of workers. The 49 workers identified include 10 engineers, 18 forestry technicians and 21 forest guards. With such a weak staff base insufficient attention is given to the socio-economic and cultural situation of local people whose livelihoods depend on resources found in the protected areas. Attempts by development agents to protect or rehabilitate ecosystems in a particular place are often contradicted by the socio-economic pressure of local people. Many laws and regulations governing land use in protected areas remain unenforced. There is the lack of adequate consultation and clarification concerning the demarcation of boundaries of protected areas as well as the limited capacity of the workers to enforce the protected area status (Jaff, 1994). All these generate conflicts and it is now being realized that the "conservationists" approach to biodiversity conservation has failed to come to grip with crucial social issues. (Ndenecho, 2005b). This approach has provoked social conflicts which often undermine the possibility of implementing and achieving basic conservation objectives. Coupled with limited human and financial resources necessary for the administration of protected areas, most forests with a reserve status often exist only on paper (Kamanda, 1994). Under these circumstances, the non-enforcement of regulations becomes an explicit strategy for the state to reduce conflicts (Figure 2 and 3).

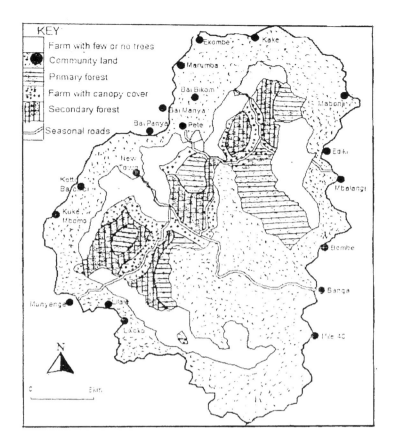

Figure 2: Degradation of the South Bakundu Forest Reserve by adjacent village communities. (Source: Effange, 2006).

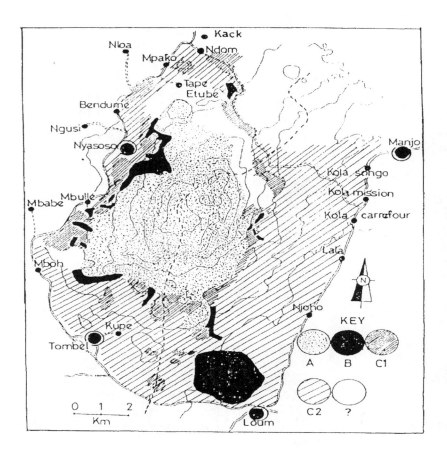

Figure 3: Degradation of Mount Kupe Forest: A = primary forest, B = secondary or disturbed forest, C1 = Farms with a less than 50% canopy cover, C2 = Farms with few or no trees, ? = Areas yet to be mapped.
(Source: Mesumbe, 2001)

Table 2: Commercial non-timber forest Products (NTFPs) in protected areas.

Name	Life form	Edible portion	Uses
Piper guineense	Climber	Seed	Flavour
Aframomum melgueta	Herb	Seed	Flavour
Aframomum logiscarpum	Herb	Seed	Flavour
Zingiber officinale	Herb	Rhizome	Flavour
Monodora myristica	Tree	Seed	Flavour
Ricino heudelotii	Tree	Seed	Flavour
Afrostynax lepidophylus	Tree	Bark	Flavour
Irvinga gabonensis	Tree	Fruit/seed	Juice/flavour
Poga oleosa	Tree	Seed	Kernel eaten
Gnetum africanum	Climber	Leaf	Vegetable
Allium cepa	Herb	Seed	Flavour
Piper nigrum	Climber	Seed	Flavour
Capsicum annum	Herb	Fruit	Flavour
Allium sativum	Herb	Bulb	Aroma
Occimum basillicum	Herb	Leaf	Aroma
Zylopia quintasii	Tree	Seed	Flavour

Source: Effange (2006) and Ewane (2006).

Table 2 above presents the commercial non-timber forest products of the study area. These products are grown in the wild. These spices and vegetables are potentially important and are capable of meeting a wide range of tastes. They are therefore gaining acceptability both on the local and world market. They are also noted for their versatility in the preparation of many local dishes and medicines. These products grow in the wild in combination with other forest trees. In fact, most of the climbing types are found climbing on forest trees as support. They are rarely cultivated but may exist as protected stands on farmlands. Occasionally, some species are introduced as intercrops with arable or cash crops. They also occur in low densities in the wild and consequently the harvested quantities are low and the prices even at local markets are high. As these species are not generally planted, they are therefore very susceptible to genetic erosion. Forest-adjacent villagers must harvest these products for a livelihood.

Table 3: Medicinal plants found in protected areas and their economic value

Plant species	Life form	Plant parts used	Observation
Aframomum spp.	Herb	Fruit, leaf, stem, seed	Sold in local and regional markets
Alstonia boonei	Tree	Bark, latex, leave	Bark sold in local markets
Ancistrocladus korupensis	Climber	Leaves	Preliminary trials by scientists for the cure of AIDS and Cancer
Annickia chlorantha	Tree	Bark, leaves	Sold in local markets
Baillonella toxisperma	Tree	Bark, seed oil	Sold in local markets
Bryophyllum pinnatum	Herb	Leaves, fruit	Not sold in markets
Canarium shweinfurthii	Tree	Fruits, seed, resin bark	Fruits sold on local markets + high value timber 40.000CFA/m³
Ceiba pentandra	Tree	Leaves, bark, root	Not sold in markets. Timber sold:
Cola spp.	Tree	Seeds, leaves, bark, roots	8000CFA/m³
Costus aferker	Herb	Stem, root, leaves, Rhizomes	Sold locally and also exported to Nigeria
Elaies guineensis	Tree	Sap, wood, leaves Oil and trunk apex	Not sold in markets Oil, kernels, and fruits sold
Eremomastax speciosa	Herb	Leaves	Generally not sold in markets
Garcinia kola	Tree	Seed, root, bark, latex	Seeds and barks sold on local markets
Garcinia mannii	Tree	Branches for chewing sticks, bark, leaves, latex	Bark sold. There is significant trade in chewing sticks
Kigelia africana	Tree		

Species	Habit	Parts used	Trade
Milicia excelsa	Tree	Buds, bark, fruits	Commonly sold in markets and regularly bought
Nuclea diderrichii	Tree	Exudates, bark, leaves, roots	Not sold, wood used for poles and furniture
Newbouldia laevis	Tree	Bark, root, fruits	Branches sold for chewing sticks.
Physostigma venenosum	Tree		Valuable timber
Piper guineensis	Shrubby Climber	Bark, root, leaves	
Prunus africanus	Woody Climber	Seeds	Sold in local markets
Pterocarpus soyauxii	Tree	Fruits, seeds, leaves, roots,	Not sold
Rauwolfia vomitoria	Tree	Bark	Commonly sold in local markets
Ricinodendron heudelotii	Tree	Stem, bark, leaves	Bark traded in world market
Senna alata	Tree		Leaves sold as vege-table, stem and bark sold
Spilanthes filicaulis	Shrub	Sap, seeds, leaves, bark	Sold for industrial transformation
Strophanthus gratus	Creeping herb	Seeds, leaf, bark, root, kernel	
Tetrapleura tetraptera	Shrub	Leaves, bark	Seeds sold widely in markets
Voacanga africana	Tree	Leaves, flowers	Not sold in markets
	Tree	Leaves, roots	Not sold in local markets
		Fruit, seeds, bark	Sold in the world market (exported)
		Seeds, latex, bark	Fruit sold as a spice. Bark not marketed
		Root	Sold to industries
			Exported

Source: Medicinal plants of the Limbe Botanic Garden (unpublished)

Table 3 above presents the medicinal and economic values of plant species found in the area. These plants play an important role in highlighting the value of all plants to mankind. Most forest adjacent communities in the area have been known, as centres of traditional healing. A variety of plant parts are harvested for medicinal purposes and are commonly traded on the local and regional markets. *Nauclea diderrichii* is sold locally in sachets for the treatment of typhoid. The money value of the timber is 8000 CFA/m³. According to forestry department statistics in Cameroon, exploitation of *Pygeum africanus* in 1990/1991 was 1,121 tons, in 1989/1990 was 1,024 tons and in 1988/1989 was 726 tons, *Pygeum* bark made up 88.6% of the plant material brought to the local pharmaceutical factory (Plantecam) in Mutengene.

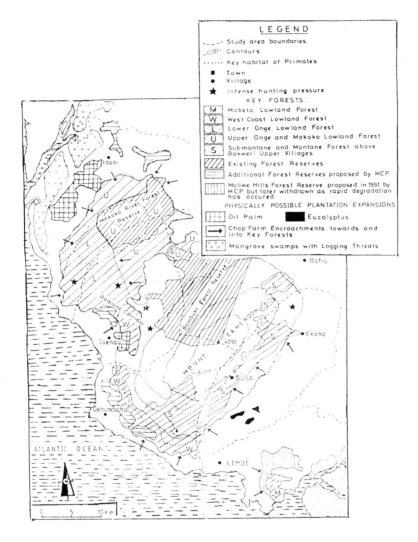

Figure 4: Local livelihoods and threats to protected areas in the Mount CameroonRegion (Source: Balgah, 2001).

Plantecam steam-dries bark and 50% is exported in powder form post-drying and the other 50% is sold as extract. The Italian Company – Invemi Delta Beffa also markets pygeum products in Europe. According to Forestry Department statistics, 1989/1990 the exploitation of *Rauwolfia vomitoria* was 15 tons. Plantecam currently exports R. vomitoria. *Strophanthus gratus* compounds. This species is exported in relatively large quantities. In 1990/91, the quantity exported was 2.7 tons.

Plantecam extracts the seed oil of *Voacanga africana* which contains vincamin for export. In 1990, forest-adjacent villages delivered 900.6 tons of seed to Plantecam Mutengene factory. *Ancistrocladus Korupensis* was first collected in the Korup National Park by botanists under contract from the United States National Cancer Institute's Natural Products Branch. It was screened for effectiveness against cancer and found to respond even better to AIDS in preliminary trials. It has thus generated international pharmaceutical interest. It has since yielded the potential anti-HIV compound michellamine b. It is, however, still too early to know whether michellamine b will pass all the tests necessary to make it into a pharmaceutical drug (Effange, 2006).

Since medicinal plants are found in the wild and mostly in concentrated stands in forest reserves, they are foraged by local people and sold to commercial companies. These commercial exploiters include Plantecam Mutengene Factory and International Transactions Trade Company in Douala. Each exploiter is assigned an area of exploitation and is prohibited from other areas. Permits are issued by the Forestry Department, stating the area of exploitation and limiting the amount of bark to be extracted. If any company exceeds the limits imposed, then it has to pay re-aforestation taxes and a fine. Despite these conditions, this sector is characterized by the corruption of forestry officials by the companies and unsustainable harvesting techniques by harvesters (forest adjacent dwellers). Natural resource management systems through protected areas and buffer zones therefore generate issues of conflict with local communities.

Table 4: Population and forest dependent livelihoods in Bamboko Forest Reserve and Bayang-Mbo Wildlife sanctuary.

Livelihood activity	Total	Protected Area		Buffer Zone	
		Number	Percentage	Number	Percentage
Hunting	885	576	65.1	309	34.9
Fishing (river fishing)	785	560	63.3	225	25.4
	889	553	62.5	332	37.5
Farming	1040	538	43.3	502	56.7
Rituals	885	347	39.2	538	60.8
Shrine/totem	885	500	56.5	385	43.5
Timber's exploitation NTFPs collection	885	770	87.0	115	13.0

Source: 2006 Fieldwork

Photo: Embraced by its mother, an infant mountain gorilla remains unaware of its precarious place in the world. In-Situ conservation in protected areas must recognize and restore land rights and autonomy in resource management to tribal minorities in order to avoid negative trends.

Table 4 indicates how the local people derive their livelihood from the forests. Livelihood activities include hunting of game, fishing, farming, timber exploitation and the collection of non-timber forest products. For the two protected areas approximately 1040 people depend on the forests for their livelihood activity. These activities are very intensive in the protected area. Natural resources in the buffer zones have been degraded through unsustainable harvesting techniques. Livelihood activities are therefore encroaching into reserves and protected areas. NTFPs collection, fishing, hunting and timber exploitation rank highest. Most people keep totems and shrines in the buffer zone. These are well protected by indigenous beliefs and traditions.

Table 5: Forest exploitation techniques per livelihood activity in Bamboko Forest Reserve and Bayang-Mbo Wildlife sanctuary

Livelihood activity	Implementation techniques	Respondents Involved	
		Number	Percentage
Poaching	▪ Guns	339	38.3
	▪ Traps	328	59.7
	▪ Others	18	2.0
Farming	▪ Slash – and – burn	889	100.0
NTFPs collection	▪ Gathering	799	90.3
	▪ Cutting/felling	18	2.0
	▪ Ring – barking	68	7.7
Totems/shrines	▪ Medicinal plants in shrine	594	69.1
		291	32.9
	▪ Animals as totom		
Timber exploitation	▪ Opening of forest roads	188	21.2
		697	78.8
	▪ Felling of trees		
Fishing (River fishing)	▪ Bamboo traps	226	25.5
	▪ Fishing nets	69	7.8
	▪ Hooks	590	66.7

Source: 2006 field work

Table 5 presents data on forest exploitation techniques per livelihood activity. Hunting involves 885 people and includes both subsistence and commercial hunting. Hunting has caused the decline in wildlife population in most protected areas (Jempa, 1995) and continued to pose a threat to the remaining populations of chimpanzee (*pan troglodytes*), drill monkeys (*Mandrillus leucophaenus*), forest buffalo (*Syncerus caffernamus*), bush pig (*Potamochoenus porcus*), giant pangolin (*Phataginuis fricupis*), and the red-eared monkey (*Cercopithecus erythrotitis*). Slash – and – burn cultivation involves 889 farmers. Sixty two percent of these farmers are encroaching on protected areas while 34% currently farm in the buffer zones. The increasing population and the need for cash is increasingly orienting the local economy from subsistence to commercial farming. NTFP collection involves unsustainable harvesting techniques. Trees are ring-barked, exposing the stems and leading to death. This constitutes a threat to the use of many medicinal plants as future resources. Tree deaths are partly due to illegal exploitation but many also are due to low wages which encourage company employees to extract as much bark as they can. The study identified 885 timber exploiters in the sites selected for study. Trees are felled and sawn using motorized saws. Timber is sold in urban markets. The opening of roads into the buffer zones and protected areas is a preliminary phase to the incursions of other forest degradation activities. The species harvested include: *Entandrophragma angolensis, Terminalia mollis, Pterocarpus soyauxii, Gibourtia tessmanni, Aninidium mannii, Entandrophragma cylondricum* and *Baillonella toxisperma*. The forest sector contribution to the gross domestic products and the weight of their exports is enormous (about 4 to 6% per year) (Effange, 2006).

Conclusion and Recommendation

Experience has shown that the most costly and least effective mechanism for enforcing rights, on the whole, is to rely on state power (Denniston, 1995; Stuart, 1986; Ndenecho, 2005). The difficulties of enforcing prohibitions on the use of state forests have been noted in many Sub-Saharan countries where most forests with protection status exist only on paper. Failure results from the fact that the rights which were denied forest-adjacent village communities were so basic to livelihoods that they were ineffective and imposed considerable social costs. Forest protection projects that ignore local livelihoods are bound to fail. This study recommends that community sanctions are the ideal mechanism for the "enforcement" through voluntary agreement of rights within fairly small and defined communities. (Tucker, 2000). They are more likely to put the local people's properties first, to be effective, and to be sustainable in economic and social terms. Arnold and Campbell (1985) summarized the many types of possible control systems which are used in traditional forest management by local communities. The control systems are elaborated using participatory approaches and enforced using indigenous religion and other traditional institutional mechanisms.

The critical issue is not so much what rules are applied, but the strength of community institutions, which set the rules and ensure that they are effective. Community sanctions are most likely to arise spontaneously and work where a cohesive social administrative structure exists. Success is likely to be achieved where there are relatively isolated village communities, little affected by migration either to or from the area. Traditional religion and well-structured socio-political institutions in the village also offer mechanisms in favour of community forest. The land, water and biological resource base of a village community can be healed through holistic wildlife management. It involves the use of practical decision-making that effectively deals with complex systems from a holistic perspective. The process should start with setting a holistic goal that ties together what people value most deeply in their lives with their life – supporting environment. Through a planning process within a holistic framework and by testing decisions against these values and the condition of the environment people can consistently make better decisions for themselves and also the fauna, flora and environment on which all live depends. This will require building human and social capital through combining training in holistic management with training related to village bank groups, forestry groups, apiculture, gardens, permaculture, game guiding, ecotourism skills, alterative income generating activities and water resource management and by demonstrating that the land can be profitably restored without compromising their values and livelihoods.

Acknowledgements

The paper acknowledges the contribution of Ewane Basil and Effange Emilia (Department of Geography, University of Buea) for the administration of questionnaires.

References

Amiet, J. L and Dowsett–Lemaire, F. (2000) Un nouveau Leptodactylodon dela Dorsale Camerounaise. (Amphibia, *Anura*). *Alytes 18:* 1 – 14

Arnold, J. and Campbell, J. (1985) collective management of hill forest in Nepal; community forestry project. Washington DC p. 7 – 15

Asong, A. (2001) Forest reserves and forest reserve strategies in South West Province. In: J. Dunlop and R. Williams (eds) *Culture and Environment*, University of Buea/University of Stratchdyde in Glasgow p. 116 – 130

Balgah, S. (2001) Exploitation and conservation of biological resources in Mount Cameron region. In: C.M. Lambi and E. B. Eze (eds). *Readings in Geography*, Unique Printers, Bamenda p. 310.324

Bawden, C. and Andrews S. (1994) Mount Kupe and its Birds. *Bulletin of African Bird Club* 1: 13 - 16

Collar, J. and Stuart S. (1988) Key forests for threatened birds in Africa. ICBP, Cambridge p. 10 – 21

Denniston, D. (1995) Sustaining mountain people and environments. Worldwatch Institute. W. W. Norton and Company, London p. 38 – 57

Effange, E. (2006) The involvement of local population in protected area management in Cameroon; Case of Bambuko Forest Reserve and Bayang-Mbo Wildlife Sanctuary. Unpublished MSc. Thesis, Dept. of Geography, University of Buea p. 60 - 78

Ewane, B. (2006) Optimising the management of dynamic ecosystems: Case of the Southern Bakundu Forest Reserve. Unpublished MSc. Thesis, Dept. of Geography, University of Buea p. 63 – 75

Dowsett, R. (1989) Preliminary natural history survey of Mambilla Plateau and some lowland forests of eastern Nigeria. *Tauraco Research Report. No. 1.* 56p

Dowsett-Lemaire, F. and Dowsett, R. (1988) Zoological survey of small mammals birds and frogs in Bakossi and Mount Kupe, Cameroon, Unpublished report for WWF – Cameroon, 46p

Dowsett-Lemaire, F. and Dowsett, R. (2000) Further biological surveys of Manenguba and Central Bakossi in March 2000, and an evaluation of the conservation importance of Manenguba, Kupe, Bakossi and Nlonako, with special reference to birds. Unpublished report for WWF – Cameroon, 45p

Fonyam, J. (2001) The legal protection of forests, a case study of Cameroon. In: J. Dunlop and R. William (eds). *Culture and Environment*, University of Buea/University of Stratchdyde in Glasgow p. 39 – 63

Fotso, R.; Dowsett-Lemaire, F.; Dowsett, R. (2001) Cameroon Ornithological club, *Birdlife Conservation Series No. 11*, ICBP, Cambridge p. 133 – 159

Gartland, S. (1989) La Conservation des ecosystemes forestiers du Cameroun. IUCN, Gland and Cambridge p. 5 – 15

Jaff, B. (1994) Management of protected areas with particular attention to poaching and cross-border cooperation in the South West Province. *Unpublished paper presented in the Regional Concertation on the Environment in Buea*, MINEF, Yaounde; March 1994. 10p.

Jongman, H. (1995) Nature conservation planning in Europe; developing ecological networks. *Landscape and Urban planning 27*: 253 – 258

Kamanda, B. (1994) The Southern Bakundu Forest Reserve Project: a rural economy survey. ITTO/ONADEF, Yaounde, p. 7 – 8

Kelkit, A., Ozxel, A. and Demirel, O. (2005) A study of the Kazdagi (Mt. Ida) National Park: an ecological approach to the management of tourism. *Int. Journal of Sustainable Development and World Ecology* 12: 1–8

McNeely, J.; Miller, K.; Reid, W.; Russel, A. and Werner, T. (1990) Conservating the World's biological diversity. IUCN/World Bank, Washington D.C. p. 11 – 12

Mesumbe, I. (2001) The ecology of Mount Kupe Forest. Unpublished Long Essay, Dept. of Geography, University of Buea. 46p

Ndenecho, E. (2005) Conserving biodiversity in Africa. Wildlife management in Cameroon. *Loyola Journal of Social Sciences 19 (2):* 211 – 228

Scatterfield, A.; Crosby, M.; Long, A.; Wege, D. (1988) Endemic bird areas of the world; priorities for biodiversity conservation. Birdlife *Conservation Series No. 7*, Cambridge p. 11 – 18

Stuart, S. N. (1986) Conservation of Cameroon Mountain Forests ICBP. Cambridge p. 12 – 19

Tucker, C. (2000) Striving for sustainable forest management in Mexico and Honduras: the experience of two communities. *Mountain Research and Development* 20: 116 – 117

White, F. (1983) The vegetation of Africa, a descriptive memoir to accompany the UNESCO/AETFAT/UNSO vegetation Map of Africa (3 plates), Allard Blom, UNESCO, Paris. Plate 1, 2 and 3. At 1:5,000,000

Chapter 5

Rural Livelihoods and the Management of National Parks

Case study: Korup National Park

Summary

Korup is a biologically lavish area in the lowland rainforest zone of Cameroon. It obtained a National Park status in 1986 and has continued to suffer from anthropogenic stresses. The study seeks to assist in ensuring a secured ecological system for inhabited protected areas using Korup as an example, that is, to assess the utilization and sustainability of socio-economic important plant species which are main sources of livelihood security in the area. This ethnobotanic study used both field and household socio-economic data obtained through the use of both open-ended questionnaire and participatory interviews. Indicators investigated included plant species, plant organs harvested, collection period, use, income value and current status. The analysis revealed 27 socio-economic species. These plants were found to contribute substantially to household income. However, there is no diversification of these products and the harvest of some is unsustainable. The non domestication and unsustainable harvest are potential indicators of long-term ecological risks which require urgent attention. Again this chapter stresses the need to integrate environment protection and livelihood concerns in conservation projects by involving and empowering local communities.

Key Words: National Park, Socio-economic important plants, Sustainable management, Anthropogenic stresses, Local livelihoods.

Introduction

Biologically, Korup is the single large lowland site in Africa for birds, butterflies and herpetofauna. It also represents a critically important site for primate conservation supporting healthy population of a number of endangered primates. Floristically, it is a centre of hyperdiversity with about 30% endemic species (KNP Management Plan, 2002 – 2007). The area is also the home to both man and biodiversity of varying plants and animals. Consequently, it is under serious anthropogenic pressure. Hunting, unsustainable harvesting of forest products and agricultural encroachment

83

are main threats. The park status was instituted in 1986 without the participatory involvement of local people in the management plan of the ecological resources. There is a need to initiate dialogue with local people and for resource managers to design policy interventions which stimulate benefits and counteract negative consequences by simultaneously considering the trade-offs between environmental protection objectives and socio-economic objectives in the processes of sustainable biodiversity conservation and management. The specific objective of this chapter is to assist in ensuring a secured ecological system for inhabited protected areas using Korup as a case study, that is, to assess the utilization and sustainability of socio-economic important plant species which are main sources of human livelihood security in the area.

Korup National Park (KNP) is located in Ndian between latitudes $4^0$54'N and $5^0$28' N; and longitudes $8^0$42'E and $9^0$16'E (Figure 1). The park is contiguous with Cross River National Park in neighbouring Nigeria. Separated only by the River Korup these two national parks protect more than 4,000km^2 of mainly lowland forest. Continued protection of the Korup forest is vital to safeguard the mangrove forests and swamps of Rio del Rey and Cross River, reputed to be the richest fishing resource in West Africa. In 1939, it was established as a "Native Administrative Forest Reserve" and in 1986 a surface area of 1,260km^2 of the forest was gazetted as the Korup National Park.

About 17% of the park is between sea level and an elevation of 120m, 49% between 120m and 360m, and 33% between 360 and 850m above sea level. Only 1% at elevations above 850m. The highest point in the park is Mount Yahan (horst). It is drained by the Bake - Munaya River which is a tributary of the Cross River, the Ndian River, the Akpasang and Korup Rivers. Studies by Gartlan (1985) identify basalts and andesites in the far north-east of the park along the banks of the Bake – Munaya River (5,000 hectares of poryphric basalt, andesite, and aporyphric basalt) of the early Tertiary or late Cretaceous period. Some salt springs have also been identified. These could be developed for tourists interest. A belt between the Ndian River and the Akpa Korup River is composed of Cretaceous sedimentary sandstone (5,000 hectares). At higher elevations, Tertiary basalts overlie the older basement rocks. Precambrian basement rock covers much of the area (113,000 hectares). It consists mainly of ectinites, quartzites and gneisses in the east; and gneisses, embrechites and syntectonic granites in the west. The Precambrian basement granite was subject to Tertiary tectonic activity resulting in a horst topography characterized by granitic boulders or castle kopjes several hundreds of metres high. These frequently contain caves and are the nesting places of the avifauna.

84

The climate is typically equatorial with a distinct dry season from December to February. The single peak wet season occurs during the rest of the year. Its flora and fauna is known to be part of the Hygrophilous Coastal Evergreen Rainforest that occurs along the Gulf of Biafra, and is part of the Cross-Sanaga-Bioko Coastal Forest Ecoregion (Olsen *et al.*, 2001). This ecoregion is considered an important centre of plant biodiversity because of its probable isolation during the Pleistocene (Davis et al., 1994) and holds an assemblage of endemic primates known as the Cameroon faunal group (Waltert *et al.*, 2002). More than 620 species of trees and shrubs have been recorded. About 30% of these are endemic. Some 480 species of herbs and climbers have also been identified. There is a variety of socio-economic plants with medicinal and food values and therefore a major source of local livelihoods.

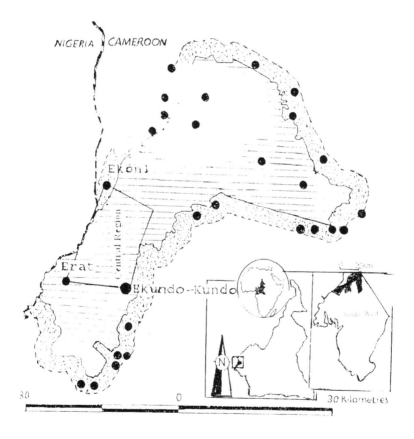

Figure 1: Location of the Korup National Park and the study area: Hachures = Korup National Park, Dotted Shades = Buffer zone, Round dots =

Forest – adjacent communities.

Records in the KNP indicate that more than 25% of all Africa's primate species are present and the area represents an important site for primate conservation. The mammal fauna consists of 33 families with 161 different species. Subsistence and commercial hunting of fauna constitutes an important source of livelihood. About 171 households living in the forest adjacent areas depend on the forest for timber and non-timber forest products. Farming is restricted by law to the immediate vicinity of the park. Typically, an average household may own 5 to 10 hectares of farmland.

Data Sources and Methodology

The data for this chapter were obtained from a combination of primary and secondary sources. The diversity, utilization and sustainability of non-timber forest products were established in both qualitative and quantitative terms after a household survey and consultations with local authorities and traditional resource users. It used an open-ended questionnaire and participatory interviews that allowed conversational two-way communication. For each plant species of importance, its abundance, status, and uses were recorded with household informants. The survey also sought to establish the collection period, contribution to household food supply, income, value, use and use status. Considering the differences in the size and composition of forest-adjacent villages, a probability proportional to the size sample, that is, multi-stage sampling methodology was adopted (clustering, stratification and simple random sampling). The sample size was 95 (age: 18 – 85 years; women 60 and men 35). A total of 171 households exist in the area of which 95 were sampled representing 55.6%. Men, women, youth and children have differing roles in collecting non-timber forest products (NTFPs) and so were proportionally represented. A market survey was carried out in the main market centre (Mundemba) to establish products traded, retail prices, and those involved.

The statistical package for the social sciences (SPSS, 13.0) and Excel 2003 were used to analyse the data. The data so obtained were supplemented by secondary data and project documents of the Korup National Park (KNP). These also were supplemented by previous studies.

Presentation of Results

Household perception of the value of NTFPs

Non-timber forest products are a significant contribution to the income and welfare of households. Respondents suggested that local NTFP collection helps them meet important household needs and sources of income such as leaves and medicinal herbs, fruits and fuelwood; while also supporting the production of secondary goods like baskets and other crafts. **Table 1**: shows that NTFP collection makes a significant contribution to household livelihood security

Table 1: Household's perception on the values of non-timber forest products

Variable	Percentage response		
	1	**0**	**n/a**
Indigenous fruits trees have medicinal values	89	7	4
Indigenous fruits trees can be intercropped with agricultural crops to provide fuel wood and external source of food supply	58	23	19
Indigenous fruit trees have amenity and ornamental values	74	12	14
Indigenous fruit trees are good source of income	98	2	0
Families depend on indigenous trees at time of food shortage	100	0	0

1 = Yes; 0 = No and N/A = I do not know

It is clear from the table that socio-economic important plant species are a major source of livelihoods and well-being to the households in the area. In general, the people surveyed believed that NTFP collection will increase with time if they are managed sustainably. This requires monitoring operations and alternative income generating sources for villagers living in and around the forest. Diversification of these resources in agricultural landscapes is also important especially for the enclave areas. Villagers believed that NTFPs provide an important source of income for sustaining their daily needs. Villagers report that their agricultural yields are under continuous threat from monkeys and other small mammals. Destruction by elephants use to be very common before the creation of the park. Most of these animals were hunted

87

before the creation of the park. NTFP collection has decreased in some areas of the park, due to dwindling resources in forests, unsustainable harvests, and reduction in demand from secondary traders.

Non-Timber Forest Products of Central KNP

A number of non-timber forest products were identified in the central zone of KNP. These are presented in table 2.

Table 2: Different use-groups of NTFP's from central KNP, their relative contributions to household income and statuses as at the year 2008

Scientific name	Local name	Part used	Use	% Contribution to household income	Status
Irvingia gabonensis (excelsor)	Bush mango	Seed	Condiment, soup	78.8	A
Garcinia cola	Bitter cola	Wood	Stimulant, medicinal	1.0	S
Piper guineensis	Bush pepper	Seed, leaf	Condiment, leaf edible	4.9	S
Oubaguia alata	Bush kernel	Seed	Edible	-	S
Tetracarpidium canophorum	Casu nut	Seed	Condiment	2	S
Cola acuminate	Country cola	Seed	Cultural	-	E
Afrostyrax lepidophyllus	Country onion	Seed, bark	Condiment	3.8	S
Cola lepidota	Monkey cola	Seed	Edible	-	A
Ricendendron heudelotti	Njansanga	Seed	Condiment	7.8	E
Poga oleosa	Shell nut	Seed	Edible	-	S
Carpolobia lutea	Hausa stick	Stem	Cattle stick	0.4	S
Garcinia mannii	Chewing stick	Wood	Dental hygiene	1.9	S
Cola nitida	Cola nut	Seed	Edible	0.4	E

Cola pachycarpa	n/a	n/a	n/a	-	S
Laccosperma secundiflorum	Rattan	Stem	Weaving	0.07	S
Eremospatha macrocarpa	Rattan	Stem	Weaving	-	S
Marantaceae	Ngongo	Leaves	Weaving, wrapping	-	E
Dacryodes edulis	Bush plum	Fruits	Edible	-	S
Aframomum spp.	Alligator pepper	Seed	Medicinal	0.3	S
Annickia chlorantha	Fever bark	Bark	Medicinal	-	S
Raphia hookeri	Raffia	Leaves	Thatching	0.7	E
Xylopia aethiopica	Ukam	n/a	n/a	-	S
Tricoscypha acuminate	n/a	n/a	n/a	-	S
Ancistrocladus korupensis	n/a	Stem	Medicinal	-	S
Treculia africana	Osakara	n/a	Edible	-	S

A: Abundant; E: Enough; S: Scarce (household survey)

Most of NTFPs are seasonal. *Irvingia gabonensis, Ricendendron heudelotti* among others, are collected mostly from June to August each year, with the highest collection often recorded in July. Eru (*Gnetum africana*) is unfortunately rare in the central region. In the peripheral zones, this product is the most important income source for households. Trade generally flourishes in the dry season when growth is luxuriant as growth is activated from October with the *reduction of soil moisture content and rains,* resulting in abundance of eru in the forest. Growth peaks in January but reduces remarkably during the rainy season between July and September, resulting in scarcity of eru in the forest. These products, together with the parts used, local names, statuses and percentage contribution to an average household income are presented (Table 2).

Distribution and Status of the Most Important Use-Groups

- **Bush mango (*Irvingia gabonensis*):** It is common around Erat and Ekon I villages. The forest around Ekundo-kundo (resettlement) area also has relatively few large-diameter individuals (dbh>10cm), indicating that there are less productive trees in these areas. This could most likely stem from over harvesting of fruits.

- *Ancistrocladus korupensis (***Ancistrocladaceae):** This woody vine is presently known only in the Korup area, within 30km west of Mundemba. It is of interest as a possible medicinal plant (Thomas, 1994) as it contains michellamine – B, a compound that does indeed show in vitro activity against HIV but also possesses significant neurotoxicity that has precluded its being advanced into clinical trials. During the study, only one species was seen in the buffer zone. However, other researchers have reported that it has only been found in the western part, the area proposed as a community forest in the resettlement area. It is important that the forest management plan for this area provides the protection of this important population and that its status is monitored.

- **Rattan palms:** Rattans are important locally for basket making and for a variety of construction purposes, including furniture. There is also a market for rattan in southern Cameroon. The central zone has both the thick *Laccosperma* and the thin *Eresmospatha* species. However, these are not abundant. Research in the resettlement area shows that these species are abundant enough (Thomas, 1994). Other commercial species of rattan include *L. secundiflorum and E. macrocarpa*, also considered abundant elsewhere in the country but rare in the central, region. Considering the species regeneration ability, and its distribution in the region, we can say that rattan is not at risk of over-harvesting. However, with the growing population, probable high demand in rattan products might exceed the carrying capacity of the environment, hence rendering it rare and even extinct. There is therefore need to encourage the cultivation of these plants.

- **Randia chewing sticks (*Massularia acuminate*):** Distribution of *Randia* is not well represented in the central zone.

- **Hausa cattle stick (*Carpolobia spp.):*** Comparatively speaking, they are not well represented in the central region of KNP.

- **Chewing stick (*Garcinia mannii*):** Also scarce and poorly represented in the region. However, it shows a healthy cumulative size-class distribution in the lowland forest, which serves as evidence of healthy regeneration and recruitment.

- **Fever bark (*Annickia chlorantha*):** Could only be identified in the buffer zone. The cumulative size-class distribution for this species exhibits good regeneration.

Sustainable Harvests of NTFPs Species

In general, NTFP exploitation that is not destructive (for example, the removal of the fruits of bush mango) can be described as relatively sustainable as long as there is evidence that the population is not declining over time through the constant removal of reproductive material (Cunningham, 1999). Destructive harvesting practices that are undertaken at low levels of exploitation such as the removal of bark strips may pose a threat to the individual, but likely not to the population or species as a whole (Table 3).

Table 3: Resource, life form, part harvested, impact of harvesting and level of sustainability

Resource	Life form	Part harvested	Impact of harvesting	Level of sustainability
Bush mango	Canopy-emergent trees	Fruits	Low	Relatively sustainable, good regeneration and community level cultivation
Carpolobia cattle stick	Small to medium tree	Stems	High	Highly unsustainable because of removal of whole stem, including root collar
Randia chewing sticks	Small to medium tree	Stem	High	Highly unsustainable, population beginning to show a significant decline
Njansanga	Canopy-emergent trees	Fruits	Low	Relatively sustainable, good regeneration
Bush pepper	Climbing	Leaves and fruits	Moderate	Relatively sustainable if leaves and fruits are plucked and the stem is not cut
Garcinia	Medium to	Bole	High	Highly sustainable,

chewing stick	large tree			species has limited geographical range and is in danger of extinction over the long term
Rattans	Climbing palms	Mature stems	Low to medium	Relatively sustainable at current levels of harvest

The Effects of Seasonality on NTFP Activities

While many non-timber forest products are available for harvest and sale all year, some are somewhat seasonal, and the economic cycle of many communities relies heavily on the timing of these resources (Table 4). The effects of seasonality are particularly pronounced for bush mango and other fruit-producing species and have significant implications for household budgets.

Table 4: Impact and seasonal distribution of non-timber forest products

Resource	Impacts of seasonality	Availability
Bush mango	High	Rainy season type (*I. gabonensis*) available July – September. Abundant in August, least in September
Carpolobia cattle stick	Low	All year, although transportation problems in rainy season restrict supply to market
Randia chewing sticks	Low	All year
Njansanga	Moderate	Fruits produced during rainy season, but after processing, they can be stored indefinitely
Bush pepper	Moderate	Fruits produced in the dry season, leaves can be harvested all year
Garcinia chewing stick	Moderate	All year, although increased availability in rainy season because of better boat access to remote creeks in forest

Bush onion	Moderate	Fruits produced during rainy season, but after drying, they can be stored for sometime

Socio-Economic Threats to the Ecological System

Hunting pressure is on-going and has greatly reduced the animal population. Apart from monkeys, it is really difficult to find other species of animals we read and hear of. The villagers also complain of a gradual decline in the quantities of Non-Timber Forest Products (NTFP's). The various activities carried out in the area and their contributions to biodiversity loss (ecological integrity) are summarized in table 5.

Table 5: Different economic activities and their impacts to ecological integrity

Activity	Extent	Impact	Permanence	Degree	Description and rationale for scoring
NTFPs collection	Scattered (2)	Moderate (2)	Permanent (4)	High (16)	Carried out by villagers in the park and environs. *Irvingia gabonensis*, for example, is highly marketable
Poaching	Scattered (2)	High (3)	Permanent (4)	Severe (24)	Drills, Monkeys and lots of other animal species. Meat could be found on sale in local restaurants

					& markets
Agriculture	Scattered (2)	Long-term (3)	Long-term (3)	High (18)	All households now engage in the cultivation of cassava, palm plantations as these products are in high demand and profitable
Fires	Localized (1)	Mild (1)	Severe (4)	Mild (4)	The use of fire for clearing agricultural lands is on the rise
Fuelwood collection	Scattered (2)	High (3)	Long-term (3)	High (18)	All households need fuel wood for cooking
Road construction	Localized (1)	Mild (1)	Short-term (1)	Mild (1)	Only footpaths are available and very localized
Settlement	Widespread (3)	Severe (4)	Long-term (3)	Severe (36)	As household and immigration increase

Note: *A separate value was assigned to each quality, and the three values were multiplied to calculate the degree of each pressure or threat. A degree of 1 to 3 was considered mild, 4 to 9 moderate, 12 to 24 high, and 27 to 64 severe.*

Demographic changes in the central zone of KNP have been fundamental. The average population growth rate, following field estimates show that it is 2% for *Ekundo-kundo* village, 4.5% at *Erat* and 2.5% for *Ekon 1* village. *Ekon 1* and *Erat* villages are very close to neighbouring Nigeria-Calabar and its environs, which also provide good markets for non-timber forest products, including animal species. Hence, apart from natural growth and positive fertility rates, the population growth in these areas can partly be explained by migration/immigration. This is posing serious threats to Korup's ecological integrity. Anthropogenic impacts such as forest conversion to agriculture, slash-and-burn cultivation threaten the ecological system. An analysis of the exploitation of timber and non-timber forest species reveals that the following taxa could be of priority conservation attention: *Afzelia africana* (Caesalpinaceae). Members of the family were generally seldom present. In particular, less than 5 stems of *Afzelia africana* were counted during the whole survey. In vegetation lexicology, one would say that it is **Vulnerable**. In the same vein, the following species can be classified as **vulnerable**: *Ancistrocladus korupensis* (Ancistrocladaceae); *Eremospatha tessmanniana*; *Diospyros crassiflora* (Ebenaceae), *Garcinia kola* (Guttiferae), *Nauclea diderichii* (Rubiaceae), *Cola flaviflora* (Sterculiaceae), *Irvingia gabonensis* (Irvingiaceae) and *Lophira alata* (Ochnaceae). Uncontrolled and destructive harvesting of non-timber forest products is having a deleterious effect on the populations of certain high-value plants (particularly *Carpolobia spp.* and *Massularia acuminate*, which belong to the Sterculiaceae). The unique biological and socio-economic nature of the region makes implementation of applied conservation and sustainable management strategies a priority. Establishment of a focused, long-term monitoring and research programme will determine the efficacy of such efforts.

Discussion and Recommendations

In terms of livelihood analyses results, the natural resources in the park are vastly more important and central to the villagers' livelihood. The communities not only collect products and continue to hunt in the park but also use the land to farm annual crops and even permanent crops like palm oil and cocoa. The villagers are more culturally and historically attached to the resources than most guards, who are viewed with great suspicion, especially if they come from the community. This combination of closeness to and dependence on the resources along with the customary proprietorship and indigenous knowledge gives the villagers greater intrinsic moral and *de facto* authority over the resources of the park.

95

Like Mbile (2009) reported, the park was created without any prior negotiations with the villages it subsumed. The authority of the poorly paid guards is only an abstraction of government policy. In the remoteness of the park, the guards lack moral, technical or traditional authority to execute their responsibilities. Similar scenarios and the effect on guards' behaviour in other protected areas are discussed by Thapar (1992) and Callister (1999), who tell a common story: the guards' insufficient psychological and material authority can create an ideal atmosphere for corruption in the form of collusion, collaboration and bribery. Though such corruption may be petty and perceived as insignificant, because it can be rampant, Callister (1999) argues, the cumulative effect on a protected area and its management can be devastating.

It should also be emphasized that there is a general lack of indigenous involvement along the marketing chain of these resources and products. The primary reason is that most communities do not have a realistic notion of the true market value of some forest products. This is particularly the case for products that are not used locally to any great extent (for example, *Randia* and *Carpolobia*). In this regard, access to the resource base, or the resource itself, is often unknowingly undersold to outside harvesters or dealers, with many communities, at best, benefiting only from the provision of labour. In addition, an inability to process and store raw materials at the community level means that only the price of raw material production accrues to the communities.

To achieve the overall aim of a more effective management of natural resources, park authorities may need to share responsibilities and, to that end, develop local capacities in resource management. Central to these two requirements is the existence of an adaptable organizational capacity and decision-making system. The traditional societies, though complex, interlink all sections of the community and can thus respond to the various needs of participatory management. It, nevertheless, requires patience to understand the traditional mechanisms of decision making and knowledge acquisition. Local communities have a build-in capacity to control harvesting as well as effectively monitor illegal felling through local arrangements, so overall livelihood costs will be lower under community management for the same level of control.

On the other hand, proper understanding of the levels of social relations in community-based resource management has important welfare implications, especially for the livelihood security of poorer households, as they should not be made worse off from institutional changes in resource management. Though this study could not compare the transaction costs of resource management under different property regimes (state, co-

96

management, community and private management), further research on comparison of transaction costs associated with different forms of property regimes may help to develop a more generalized theory of transaction costs and their significance in managing the local commons. There is also a need to domesticate and integrate these useful plants in local farming systems.

The heavy reliance on just a few forest resources for income can pose considerable hardship for some communities. NTFP's in central Korup contribute over 70% household food supply during the planting season. The central region is primarily dependent on the bush mango resource for access to the cash economy, leaving villagers vulnerable during years of poor production. This shows that in the event of a very poor crop yield, perhaps due to attack by pests, famine may be brought to the region. Product diversification would make a huge difference in these villages and others that also rely on two or three key products. There is great need for agricultural diversification to include these products on farmlands. Already in the Korup areas, some Common Initiative Groups are trying to domesticate eru (*Gnetum africana*) which is one of the greatest NTFPs in international markets. The encouragement of such activities by government will not only ensure the livelihood security of the people, but will go a long way to reduce the current pressure on the entire ecological system. There is need to develop alternative sources of income generation.

Diversity is the very basis of ecological security. Diversity is the very basis of resilience and sustainability. Monocultures are usually vulnerable and liable to be destroyed. Monocultures – whether in social, cultural, anthropogenic, or in biological terms – are dangerous, unsustainable and their maintenance costs the Earth. A plan for diversification is a liability in the Korup region at least for sustainability and ecological security of the area.

Acknowledgments

This chapter is the contribution of Dr. Innocent Ndoh Mbue (PhD Environmental Science, School of Environmental Sciences, China University of Geosciences).

References

Callister, J.D. (1999) Corrupt and illegal activities in the forestry sector: current understandings and implications for World Bank Forest Policy. World Bank Paper (http.//www/fao.org/DOCREP/ 003/YO900e 18.htm), assessed on March 16th, 2009.

Cunningham, A. (1994) The management of the non-wood forest products in protected areas: Lessons of a case study in multiple-use in Bwindi Impenetrable National Park Uganda. In: T.C.H. Sunderland, L. C. Clark, P. Vantomme (eds). *Non-timber forest products of Africa: Current Research issues and prospects for conservation and development.* F.A.O. Rome.

Davis, S.D.; Heywood, V.H.; Hamilton, A.C. (1994) Centres of plant biodiversity: a guide and strategy for their conservation. *Volume 1,* IUCN Publication Unit, Cambridge.

Gartlan, J.S. (1985) The Korup regional management plan: conservation and development in the Ndian Division of Cameroon. *WWF/IUCN Project Report No. 3206.*

Mbile, P. (2009) The Korup National Park story revisited. In: Diaw, M.C.; Aseh, T. and Prabhu, R. (eds). *In search of common ground: adaptive collaborative management of forests in Cameroon.* Centre for International Forestry Research, Bogor, Indonesia.

Olsen and Folke (2001) Local ecological knowledge and institutional dynamics for ecosystem management: a study of Lake Racken watershed, *Ecosystems vol. 4,* p. 85 – 104.

Thapar, V. (1992) The tiger's destiny. Kyle Cathie, London.

Thomas, W. (1994) Preliminary botanical inventory of the Tabe Road Resettlement Area. Report of GTZ and Korup Project.

Waltert, M.; Lien; Faber, K.; Muhlenberg, M. (2002) Further declines of threatened primates in the Korup project area, South West Cameroon, *Oryx vol. 36,* p. 257 – 265.

Chapter 6

Contribution of Non-Timber Forest Products to Household Revenue: In Forest-Adjacent Communities

Case Study: Takamanda Forest Reserve

Summary

The use of non-timber forest products (NTFPs) in the tropical rainforest management has received greater attention over the past two decades. They are collected from a wide range of ecotypes such as high forest, farm fallows, otherwise disturbed forest, and farmland for use as medicine, food and barter. People throughout the tropics rely on their harvest and sale for their economic well-being. The chapter uses a combination of primary and secondary data to enhance an understanding of the evolutionary process in non-timber forest product collection and the factors that contribute to the intensification of the harvesting of products, the ethnobotanic and socio-economic characteristics, the factors affecting availability, and sustainability. The chapter concludes that non-timber forest product production is mainly limited to extraction from natural forests although there is a growing interest to domesticate and cultivate the most economically viable species. The intensification of collection and the tendency towards domestication depends on both supply and demand factors. Supply factors include seasonality, regeneration rates, the population of individual species in various ecotypes, ease of access to collectors, as well as access to labour. The demand factors include access to markets and the prices of products. The chapter posits that these factors influence the dynamics of non-timber forest product production and management. The current rate of harvesting economically viable species exceeds the ability of the species to regenerate, and the harvest of a number of species can be regarded as unsustainable. It therefore examines the constraints pertaining to their sustainable and equitable exploitation.

Key Words: Non-timber forest products, availability, harvest, intensification, domestication, sustainability, rainforest.

Introduction

Non-timber forest products (NTFPs) have emerged as a vital income-generating activity in many parts of the world. This has raised concerns of their ecological sustainability (Tewari and Campbell, 1995). Since the early 1990s increased attention has been given to the extraction of non-timber forest products from natural forests as a means of reconciling rural development and environmental conservation (den Hertog and Wiersum, 2000; Bhatt *et al.*, 2000). Consequently, evaluation of the socio-economic characteristics of non-timber forest product production and assessment of the potential of non-timber forest product extraction for sustained management of natural forests has become an important focus of research (Ros-Tonen *et al*, 1995); Ruiz-Perez and Arnold, 1996). Non-timber forest products are materials derived from forests – excluding timber but including the following: bark, roots, tubers, corms, leaves, flowers, seeds, fruits, sap, honey, resin, fungi, and animal products (Sunderland *et al.*, 2003).

To enhance understanding of the evolutionary processes in non-timber forest product collection and the factors that contribute to intensification of the harvesting of products, a case study of the ethnobotanic and socio-economic characteristics of non-timber forest products in Takamanda rainforest is presented here. The study identifies the different plant non-timber forest products, plant organs exploited, contribution to the household income, marketing channels and the factors affecting availability and sustainability.

The study therefore seeks to identify the major non-timber forest products, the plant parts exploited and their contribution to the household economy. It examines the basic hypothesis that the extraction of non-timber forest products is a first stage in a process of the gradual domestication of these species which presently suffer from seasonal availability and are threatened by unsustainable harvesting. Domestication is therefore a response to the problem of the availability of these products in the wild. There is a need to regulate the collection of these products and to promote their integration in local farming systems.

Cameroon extends from 2^0N to 13^0N latitude and between $8^0$25'E and $16^0$20'E longitude. The study area is located in the South West Province of Cameroon and is part of the Guino-Congolian forest which has an approximate land surface area of 2.8 million km^2. Rainfall in this vast forest varies from 1500 to 10.000mm per year, giving rise to a variety of vegetation floristic regions (White, 1983). The region contains 84% of known primates, 68% of known African passerine birds, and 66% of known African butterflies (Groombridge and Jenkins, 2000). For this reason, the Guino-

Congolian rainforest is an important focal point for conservation efforts in Africa (Sunderland *et al.* 2003).

Takamanda forest is located between latitudes 5^0 59' and 6^0 21'N and longitudes 9^0 11' and 9^0 30'E. It has a land area of 67,599 hectares in the Cross River Valley along the eastern border of Nigeria (Gartlan, 1989). Much of the lowland area in the southern and central parts of the forest is rolling terrain between 100 and 400m above sea level. It rises sharply to an altitude of 1500m in the northern part. The Cross River and its numerous tributaries drain the area (Figure 1). In general, the area has two distinct seasons with most rainfall occurring from April to November, peaking in July and August with a second peak in September with a total annual rainfall of up to 4500mm. the climate is mainly dry from November to April. January and February usually receive no rainfall. The mean annual temperature is 27^0C and the wet season is cooler than the dry season.

There are 43 villages within and around the forest, including 12 villages on the Nigerian side of the border, with a total population of 15, 0707 inhabitants (Schmidt – Soltau *et al.*, 2001). Letouzey (1985) estimates that the human population density is between 6 to 12 inhabitants per km^2. The dominant tribe is the Anyang, and the main spoken language is Denya. The forest was gazetted as a forest reserve in 1934. As with all gazetted areas in Cameroon, the reserve is managed at the national level by the Cameroon Ministry of Environment and Forests (MINEF). During gazettement of the reserve, local populations were granted traditional rights to use the forest for their subsistence-based livelihoods. They also have legal rights of passage through the Takamanda Forest Reserve (TFR), and the main travel route is the basis of a strong cross-border trading pattern. Agriculture, hunting, fishing, lumbering, and the gathering of non-timber forest products are widespread throughout the reserve (Mdaihli *et al.*, 2003).

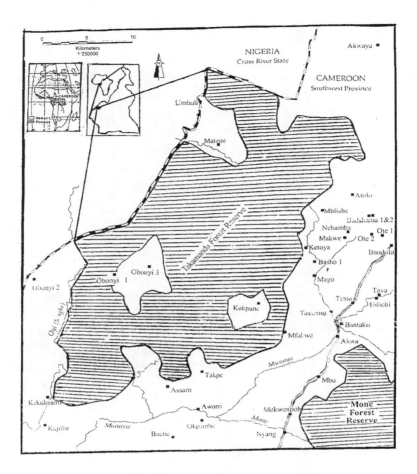

Figure 1: *Location of the Takamanda Forest Reserve and the forest-adjacent villages.*

Research Methods and Data Sources

The study consisted of a series of semi-structured and informal interviews with resource users and technical staff of the Takamanda Forest Reserve, an inventory - based resource assessment by the botanist of the reserve, and market surveys.

A series of semi-structured interviews - employing an open - format that allowed conversational, two-way communication – was undertaken in the villages of Kajifu, Takamanda, Obonyi 1, Obonyi III, Matene, Mblishi and Nfakwi (Figure 1). In each village, the interviews were conducted mainly with resource users of key non-timber forest products. The users included women and youths.

The resource inventory involved four community – managed forest areas, that is Takamanda, Obonyi I, Matene and Mfakwi (Figure 1). The objective was to identify the useful plants and the plant organs exploited. In common with tested methodology for non-timber forest products in the Takamanda Forest Reserve area established by Sunderland and Tchouto (1999). The inventory consisted of a series of temporary, parallel, 10m-wide transects established along a base-line at predetermined intervals of 100m (10% sampling). Each transect was 1km in length along a pre-determined compass bearing. The goal is to include a full range of forest types along the length of each transect.

Once the transects were established, the enumeration team led by the botanist of the reserve moved slowly along the transect and carefully searched within 5m either side of the central line for individuals of all species selected for the inventory. The 5m distance was checked with a tape. The information was recorded on field work sheets along with the location of the transects. Additional information included the vernacular name, common name, main uses, plant parts exploited and evidence of harvest.

This was followed by informal market surveys at Mbu, Nyang, Mukonyong, Eshobi and Mamfe. These surveys provided a useful overview of products being traded and their contribution to the household income. Seasonal patterns of availability on markets and the impact of harvesting on the sustainability of non-timber forest products in the area were obtained from secondary data sources (Sunderland *et al*; 2003).

Results and Discussions

The forest management condition in Takamanda Forest Reserve is rather complex. Although a government owned forest, it is controlled *de facto* by local forest user groups (FUGs). Regardless of legal title, the forest is treated by local people as a common property resource. Forest officials and villages have two opposing (and sometimes conflicting) views of access rights in the forest. On the one hand forest officials claim authority over the land and frequently take action against unauthorized collection of forest products, while accepting (within limitations) that forest-adjacent villages are breaching the law. On the other hand, indigenous FUGs make their own decisions about forest use while acknowledging that MINEF does impose controls. Existing legislation on forest management at community level has no provision for non-timber forest products. Aside from permits issued by MINEF for the transport and evaluation of *Gnetum africana* (eru), many non-timber forest products, no matter their market value, are not included in the current permit system, which focuses primarily on medicinal plants.

103

However, MINEF recently created a department for non-timber forest products charged with formalizing revenue collection from the non-timber forest product sector. To date, no policy changes have been proposed.

Table 1: Non-timber forest products of the *Takamanda Forest Reserve* and their local names

No	Non-timber forest products	Species name	Vernacular names
1	Bush mango	*Irvingia gabonensis* and *I.wombolu*	bush mango (vern); ogbono (Igbo); bojep (Boki); eloweh (Ovande); kelua (Basho); gluea (Anyang)
2	Eru	*Gnetum africanum* and *Gnetum buchholzianum*	eru (Efik); eru (Ibibio); ukasi (Igbo); ikokoh (Ovande); gelu (Anyang); ecole (Boki)
3	*Carpolobia* (cattle sticks)	*Carpolobia alba* and *C. lutea*	cattle stick (vern); sanda (Hausa); nyerem-mbe (Ovande); okah (Boki); essa (Anyang); fesha (Basho)
4	*Randia* (chewing sticks)	*Massularia acuminate(Randia)*	Randia chewing stick (vern); pako (Yoruba); odeng (Boki); egili (Ovande); egili (Anyang); feyili (Basho)
5	Njansang	*Ricinodendron heudelotti*	njansang (vern); ngoku (Basho); itche (Becheve); ngoge (Boki); ngongeh (Anyang)
6	Bush pepper	*Piper guineensis*	kakwale (Ovande); iyeyeh (Becheve); ashoesie (Boki); taquale (Basho); acachat (Anyang)
7	*Garcinia* (chewing sticks)	*Garcinia mannii*	Igbo chewing stick (vern); osun ojie (Boki); okok (Efik); aku ilu (Igbo)
8	Bush onion	*Afrostyrax kamerunensis*	felou (Basho); elonge (Becheve); eloweh (Ovande); elu (Anyang)
9	Njabe oil	*Baillonella toxisperma*	moabi (Trade); bojie = stump, edjie = fruits (Boki); mpoh (Basho)
10	Rattan canes	*Laccosperma secundiflorum, L. robustum* (large diameter), *Eremospatha macrocarpa* (small diameter)	gekwiya (Anyang) = large rattan; echie (Anyang) = cane ropes
11	Fever bark	*Annickia chlorantha*	kakerim (Boki); foukou (Basho); ekwoh (Anyang); ofaechi (Becheve)

104

Source: 2008 Fieldwork

Table 1 presents an inventory of important non-timber forest products in Takamanda Forest Reserve. The forest-adjacent villages have a long tradition of collecting non-timber forest products as a source of income, for barter and subsistence. The exact number of households involved in their collection is yet to be assessed. It is however an important household activity. Non-timber forest products help to stabilize household incomes because they can be harvested when demand for farm labour is low but when non-timber forest product production is at its peak (Schmidt-Soltau, 2001). It is estimated that 70% of the total population in the area collects forest products for consumption and sale, representing an estimated income of about 850.000 U. S. dollars a year (Ayeni and Mdaihli, 2001), or a mean of 320 U. S. dollars per household. This constitutes 39% of total household income. Some studies also estimate that the majority (68%) of harvested non-timber forest products are sold in home communities, 19% are transported for sale in Nigeria, and 13% are traded in local Cameroon markets (Schmidt – Soltau, 2001; Sunderland, 2001).

Table 2: Takamanda forest non-timber forest products, main markets and their contribution to the average household economy of forest adjacent villages

No	Common name	Scientific name	Main uses	Percentage contribution to cash income per household	Main market(s)
1	Bush mango	*Irvingia gabonensis* and *I. wombolu*	Condiment, soup thickener	58.9	Ikom, Amana (Nigeria) Mamfe
2	Eru	*Gnetum africanum* and *G. buccholzianum*	Edible vegetable	23.3	Ikom, Amana (Nigeria) Mamfe
3	Njansang	*Ricinodendron heudelotii*	Condiment	6.6	Mbu, Nyang, Mamfe
4	Bush pepper	*Piper guineensis*	Condiment, leafy vegetable	2.9	Ikom, Amana (Nigeria) Mamfe
5	Chewing	*Garcinia mannii*	Dental	1.9	Agbokim, Ikom

			hygiene		(Nigeria) Mamfe
	stick				
6	Bush onion	*Afrostyrax kamerunensis*	Condiment	1.5	Ikom, Amana (Nigeria) Mamfe
7	Bitter kola	*Garcninia kola*	Stimulant medicinal	1.0	Mbu, Nyang, Mamfe
8	Raffia	*Raphia hookeri*	Thatching	0.7	Local sale within TFR
9	Hausa stick	*Carpolobia lutea* and *C. alba*	Cattle stick	0.4	Ikom (Nigeria)
10	Cola nut	*Cola nitida*	Stimulant, cultural use	0.4	Ikom, Amana (Nigeria) Mamfe
11	Alligator pepper	*Aframomum spp.*	Medicinal	0.3	Mbu, Nyang, Mamfe
12	Akpa	*Tetrapleura tetraptera*	Condiment	0.1	Mamfe
13	Njabe	*Baillonella toxisperma*	Oil	0.1	Local sale, Mamfe
14	Essok	?	Edible	0.1	Unknown
15	Screw pine	*Pandanus candelabrum*	Thatching for mats	0.07	Local sale within TFR
16	Rattan	*Laccospernia secundiflorum, L. robustum and Eremospatha macrocarpa*	Weaving	0.07	Local sale within TFR
17	Ngongo	*Marantaceae*	Weaving, wrapping	0.06	Local sale within TFR
18	Bush plum	*Dacryodes edulis*	Edible	0.06	Local sale within TFR
19	Poga	*Poga oleosa*	Edible	0.06	Local sale within TFR

Source: 2008 Fieldwork and archival material of Takamanda Forest Reserve

Table 2 presents the commercial non-timber forest products, their uses, main markets and contribution to household incomes. (Schmidt-Soltau, 2001; Sunderland, 2001). *Irvingia gabonensis* and *Irvingia wombolu* (bush mango), and *Gnetum africana* and *Gnetum buccholzianum* (eru) combined contribute to 82% of household income. These are the most valuable non-timber forest products in terms of the local livelihoods they support. *Carpolobia lutea* and *Carpolobia alba* (Cattle stick) and Rattan used in weaving handicraft have a relatively high retail value. Prior to the early 1980s non-timber forest products had very little economic value as these were head-loaded to local markets with little spheres of influence. Increasing improvement in access to markets south of the reserve by 1990 facilitated greater access to the local resources. This resulted in a corresponding increase in the harvest and sale of non-timber forest products by both indigenous people and invading Nigerians (Ebot, 2001). This has intensified the harvesting of *Gnetum spp. Carpolobia spp.*, and *Garcinia mannii* to the extent that over-exploitation has been sensed.

Figure 2: *Some* non-timber forest products of the ***Takamanda Rainforest:***
    A = Five kinds of caffeine-rich cola and their leaves. Cola nuts make up a prized trade commodity.
    B = Stripping the bark from a tree for a spice (*bush onion*)
    C = Ripe pepper berries await harvest (*bush pepper*)
    D = Mushrooms springing up among mosses competing for a stump draw nourishment from decayed wood

Table 3: Non-timber forest products of the Takamanda Forest Reserve, their uses, and plant organs exploited

No	Scientific name	Plant part used
1	*Irvingia gabonensis* and *L. wombolu*	Seed
2	*Gnetum africanum* and *G. buccholzianum*	Leaves
3	*Ricinodendron heudelotii*	Seed
4	*Piper guineensis*	Seed, leaf
5	*Garcinia mannii*	Wood
6	*Afrostyrax kamerunensis*	Seed
7	*Garcinia kola*	Seed
8	*Raphia hookeri*	Leaves
9	*Carpolobia lutea* and *C. alba*	Stems
10	*Cola nitida*	Seed
11	*Aframomum spp.*	Seed
12	*Tetrapleura tetraptera*	Seed pod
13	*Baillonella toxisperma*	Seed
14		Mushroom
15	*Pandanus candelabrum*	Leaves
16	*Laccosperma secundiflorum L. robustum* and *Eremospatha macrocarpa*	Stems
17	*Marantaceae*	Leaves
18	*Dacryodes edulis*	Fruits
19	*Poga oleosa*	Seed

Source: 2008 Fieldwork

Table 4: Seasonality patterns for some key non-timber forest products of the **Takamanda forest**

No	Non-timber forest product	Impacts of seasonality	Availability
1	Bush mango	High	Rainy season type *(I. gabonensis)* available June to September; dry season type *(I. wombolu)* available February to April
2	Eru	Moderate	All year, although there is less plucking and reduction of supply during early rains as people are occupied with farming
3	Carpolobia (cattle sticks)	Low	All year, although transportation problems in rainy season restrict supply to markets
4	Randia (chewing sticks)		All year, although transportation problems in rainy season restrict supply to markets
5	Njansang	Moderate	Fruits produced during rainy season, but after processing, they can be stored indefinitely
6	Bush pepper	Moderate	Fruits produced in dry season, leaves can be harvested all year
7	Garcinia (chewing sticks)	Moderate	All year, although increased availability in rainy season because of better boat access to remote creeks in forest
8	Bush onion	Moderate	Fruits produced during the rainy season, but after drying, they can be stored for some time
9	Njabe oil	Moderate	Fruits produced in early rains; oil can be stored indefinitely

Source: Archival material of the Takamanda Forest Reserve

Table 3 presents the major non-timber forest products, the plant organs exploited. The condiments and soup thickeners such as bush mango, Njansang, bush pepper, bush onion and the seed pod of *Tetrapleura tetraptera* (Nkpa) are dried as a means of preservation for the market. *Aframomum sp.* is medicinal and is either sold fresh or dried, leafy vegetables are sold dried while edible fruits are sold fresh. The seeds that are stimulants are preserved in a cold and dry environment to cure before eventual sale. The non-timber forest product sector is still very traditional with little knowledge of value addition. To achieve optimum benefits, value addition can aid the rural economy. If these products collected from the wild can be processed local people can realize greater benefits. The products therefore do not generate many benefits to forest users because they do not have adequate knowledge of or access to improved processing, packaging technologies, and marketing. There is however the potential for the government, rural development agency, and non-governmental organization incentives to promote small-scale village enterprises that could greatly increase rural people's incomes. Processing and preservation of products will also alleviate the problems associated with seasonal availability. Such measures can also help to reduce over-harvesting and promote conservation. The processing of spices and condiments is gradually gaining ground in urban centres but not to the interest of forest users, sustainable harvesting and conservation efforts.

Table 4 presents the dynamics of non-timber forest products. According to Ebot (2001), during the last decade, the harvesting of products has increased considerably. The main reason for the intensification of collection has been the considerable increase in the price of non-timber forest products in urban markets such as Mamfe, Bamenda, Douala, Kumba and Limbe. Cross-border trade with Nigeria has also increased. Another factor influencing intensification is the changing labour situation. Villagers are involved in seasonal agricultural work and therefore growing dependence on off-farm income. This increases the amount of time they have for collecting non-timber forest products from the wild, causes over-exploitation and raises the labour cost. It should be worthwhile to invest some labour in establishing non-timber forest product stands in fallow fields, farmlands and private forests. Intensification of harvesting is also influenced by the effects of seasonality. While many non-timber forest products are available for harvest and sale all year round, some are somewhat seasonal, and the economic cycle for many communities relies heavily on the timing of these resources (Table 4). The effects of seasonality are particularly pronounced for bush mango and fruit-producing species and have significant implications for household budgets. Local people are consequently gradually establishing bush mango and *Njansang* plantings.

Tree growing for non-timber forest products is likely to evolve through a number of definable common stages. Where forest cover is locally abundant and population densities are low, tree management exists, but is usually passive. The off-take of tree-based products is usually offset by natural regeneration and tree growth. As population pressure increases, farmers may respond by leaving more trees during land clearance and by more intensively managing the remaining trees by practices such as coppicing, pollarding and pruning, which result in higher total production. As tree resources become increasingly scarce, farmers may take measures to stimulate tree regeneration (Arnold, 1995). This should not be conceived as a discrete activity but rather as the first stage in the process of gradual domestication of non-timber forest product species.

Table 5: The impact of harvesting of key non-timber forest products and implications for sustainability in Takamanda Forest Reserve

No	Non-timber forest products	Life form	Part harvested	Impact of harvesting	Level of Sustainability
1	Bush mango	Canopy-emergent tree	Fruits	Low	Relatively sustainable, good regeneration and community-level cultivation
2	Eru	Woody liana	Leaves	Medium to high (depending on technique)	Relatively sustainable if leaves are plucked and the stem is not cut, but destructive unsustainable harvesting is often undertaken
3	Njansang	Canopy-emergent tree	Fruits	Low	Relatively sustainable, good regeneration and community-level "encouragement"
4	Carpolobia (cattle sticks)	Small to medium tree	Stems	High	Highly sustainable because of removal of whole stem, including root collar
5	Garcinia (chewing stick)	Medium to large tree	Bole	High	Highly unsustainable; species has limited geographical range and is in danger of extinction over the long

111

					term
6	Randia (chewing stick)	Small to medium tree	Stems	High	Highly unsustainable; population beginning to show a significant decline
7	Njabe	Canopy-emergent tree	Fruits (more commonly timber)	Low to high	Relatively sustainable if harvested for fruits, but unsustainable if harvested for timber
8	Bush pepper	Climbing	Leaves and fruits	Moderate	Relatively sustainable if leaves and fruits are plucked and the stem is not cut
9	Rattan canes	Climbing plants	Mature stems	Low to medium	Relatively sustainable at current levels of harvest

Source: Archival material of the Takamanda Forest Reserve

Table 5 presents the impact of exploitation intensity and its implications on the sustainability of non-timber forest products. But for *Carpolobia spp., Gnetum spp., Garcinia, Randia* and *Baillonella toxisperma,* the impact of harvesting is low and relatively sustainable. *Massularia acuminata (randia)* suffers from over-exploitation of larger individuals and poor regeneration due to the removal of mature individuals. Exploitation therefore has a long-term effect on the population. There is also the over-exploitation of *Carpolobia spp.* in higher elevations such as Obonyi I and Mfakwe. Mature individuals occur in low densities. Despite healthy regeneration on most sites, the clear absence of larger diameter individuals due to harvesting and removal will certainly affect long-term viability of the population. *Garcinia spp.* used for dental hygiene (chewing stick) is poorly represented at higher-elevations indicating the impact of over-exploitation. There are many reports of local scarcity of *Gnetum spp.* (eru) in areas with greater access to markets.

Destructive harvesting practices that are undertaken at low levels of exploitation such as the removal of bark strips (for example, *Annickia chlorantha)* may pose a threat to individual plants but likely not to the population or species as a whole (table 5). In general, many non-timber forest products such as *bush mango, njansang, bush onion,* and *bush pepper,* where the harvesting are minimal, are not at immediate risk of being over-exploited, and there are few reports of increasing scarcity of these products (Mgbe, 2008). Destructive harvesting such as felling and removal of individuals is wholly unsustainable. In terms of conservation, over-exploitation is

112

exacerbated when a species occurs in low densities or has a restricted natural distribution such as *Garcinia mannii*. Under such circumstances harvesters must travel deep into the forest or farther and farther into the forest to find desired products. The problem is also exacerbated by agricultural encroachment into the forest.

For key resources such as *eru* and *bush mango* the majority of villages have clear traditional controls on collection from their village forestlands. They exclude "outsiders". The harvest of other non-timber forest products requires the payment of a token fee to the traditional village institution. Nevertheless, local people do not derive substantial benefits from the non-timber forest product resources because they do not know the actual market – value of the products at the final point-of-sale. A key issue in the control of non-timber forest product resources is the lack of capacity within MINEF. This agency suffers from shortfalls in staff expertise, inadequate basic infrastructure, and logistical support to implement much of the formal forestry legislation.

After an initial stage of open-access extraction from natural forest, there is need for the newly instituted non-timber forest product department of MINEF to control utilization through the definition and control of user rights. These access and control measures should gradually be oriented towards biological practices such as purposeful protection, stimulation of tree growth and production and propagation. For example, community level initiatives at planting *bush mango* have proved successful. There is also an interest to cultivate *eru*. The control of collection techniques in the wild can ensure a sustainable future supply, while the setting of opening dates for collection of non-timber forest products can allow efficient labour investment, higher yield, better quality of products, and a fair distribution of benefits among forest users. The cultivation of non-timber forest products, promotion of local processing and the organization of markets can further production efficiency. These measures should be accompanied by product diversification at the village level in order to avoid heavy reliance on some non-timber forest products and the vulnerability of households in time or season of scarcity.

Conclusions

Rainforests support numerous livelihoods for the rural poor in the tropics. The data shows that non-timber forest product production is mainly limited to extraction from natural forests although there is a growing interest to domesticate and cultivate the most economically important species. The paper also demonstrates that intensification of collection and the tendency towards domestication depends on both supply and demand factors. The supply or availability of non-timber forest products includes ecological factors, such as natural occurrence, seasonality, and ease of access to the species concerned, as well as access to labour. The demand factors include access to markets and the prices. Considering the effects of these factors on the dynamics of non-timber forest product collection and management, the study suggests that extraction of non-timber forest products from natural forests should not be conceived as a discrete activity but rather as the first stage in the process of gradual domestication of valuable non-timber forest product species in view of their importance to household incomes. The current rate of harvest of economically important species exceeds the ability of the species to regenerate, and the harvest of a number of species can be regarded as unsustainable. These include *Carpolobia, Massularia accuminata, Garcinia,* and *Gnetum spp.* There may also be long-term adverse effects on regeneration from seed removal of *Irvingia Spp.* and the plucking of *Gnetum* leaves for vegetable. Apart from domestication efforts there is an urgent need to devise guidelines for the sustainable management of high-value non-timber forest products. Product diversification and research on new non-timber forest product resources could help reduce the current pressure on available resources of the rainforest. There are significant options for enhancing the income generating potential of these non-timber forest resources through value-addition, and the regulation of harvesting.

Acknowledgements

The author acknowledges with thanks the participation of Mgbe Selestin Tabi in the field phase of the study.

References

Arnold, J. E. M. (1995) Framing the issues. In: J. E. M. Arnold and P. A. Dewees (eds). Tree management in farmer strategies: responses to agricultural intensification. Oxford University Press, Oxford, p. 3 – 17

Ayeni, J. O. S. and Mdaihli, M. (2001) Cameroonian – German (MINEF – GTZ) project for the promotion of forests around Akwaya. *Project Planning Workshop*, PROFA, Mamfe.

Bhatt, I. D.; Ranbeer, S. R. and Dhar, U. (2000). The availability, fruit yield, and harvest of *Myrica esculenta* in Kumaun (West Himalaya), India. *Mountain Research and Development vol. 20, No. 2,* p. 146 – 153 den Hertog, W. H. and Wiersum, K. F (2000). Timur *Zanthoxylum armatum*, production in Nepal: dynamics in nontimber forest resource management. *Mountain Research and Development, vol. 20, No. 2*, p. 136 – 145.

Ebot, R. (2001) Project for the protection of forest around Akwaya. *PROFA Planning Workshop*. PROFA, Mamfe: 8th – 13th May, 2001.

Gartlan, S. (1989) La conservation des ecosystèmes forestiers du Cameroun. *IUCN Programme Pour les Forêts Tropicales*. Gland, Switzerland.

Groombridge, B. and Jenkins, M. D. (2000) Global biodiversity: Earth's Living Resources in the 21st Century. *UNEP – World Conservation Monitoring Centre*, Cambridge.

Letouzey, R. (1985) Notice de la carte phytogéographie du Cameroun: Institut de la Carte Internationale de la végétation, Toulouse.

Mgbe, S. T. (2008) The socio - economic impact of the Takamanda Forest Reserve on the adjacent forest communities. Unpublished long-essay, Dept. of Geography, E. N. S. Bambili, University of Yaounde I, 43p.

Ros – Tonen, M.; Djksma, W. and Lammerts van Bueren, E. (1995)Commercial and sustainable extraction of nontimber forest products: towards a policy and management-oriented research strategy. Tropenbos Foundation, Wageningen.

Ruiz – Perez, M. and Arnold, J. E. M. (1996) Current issues in nontimber forest products research. Centre for International Forestry Research, CIFOR, Bogor.

Schmidt – Soltau, K. (2001) Human activities in and around the Takamanda Forest Reserve. Unpublished Report for PROFA, Mamfe

Sunderland, T.C. and Tchouto (1999) A participatory survey and inventory of non-timber and timber forest products of the Mokoko River Forest Reserve, South West Province, Cameroon. Unpublished report for USAID/CARE.

Sunderland, T. C. H. (2001) Cross River State community forest project. Nontimber Forest Products' Advisor Report. Monitoring and Assessment of Biodiversity Programme (SI/MAB) Washington D. C.

Sunderland, T. C. H.; Comisky, J. A. and Sunderland, J. L (2003) Takamanda: the biodiversity of an African rainforest. Smithsonian National Zoological Park. (SI/MAB),Washington D. C, p. 155 – 172

Tewari, D. D. and Campbell, J. Y. (1995) Developing and Sustaining non-timber forest products: some policy issues and concerns with special reference to India: *Journal of Sustainable Forestry vol. 3*, No. 1, p. 53 – 79

White, F. (1983) The vegetation of Africa. UNESCO, Paris.

Chapter 7

Forest-User Groups and Forest Dependent Livelihoods in Community Forests

Case Study: Oku Mountain Forest

Summary

It is now being realized by development agencies that using state power to enforce protection status for forests has failed to come to grips with crucial social issues and has provoked conflicts which often undermine the possibility of implementing and achieving basic conservation objectives. This approach ignores the livelihoods of forest adjacent communities. The search for new wildlife management models has yielded the community forest management concept. The chapter appraises the implementation of this concept. It identifies the forest-dependent livelihoods and their impacts on the sustainability of the resource by using an ethnobotanical survey and a forest damage assessment rating. Group interviews of forest management institutions identified the constraints of the model from the perspective of traditional communities. The study concludes that community forest management is yet to resolve the problem of forest resource depletion due to socio-economic and political constraints and the lack of local institutional capacities to enforce management regulations and plans. Finally, it identifies the scope for supporting and strengthening existing structures and institutions and creating new ones as a basis for enforcing management plans and regulations.

Key Words: Sustainable management, forest-dependent livelihoods community forest management model, implementation constraints, strategies and control systems.

Introduction

Mountain areas are examples of less recognized regions with critical types of biodiversity (Roy, 2001). Mountain dwellers typically live on the economic margins as nomads, part-time hunters and foragers, small farmers and herders, blacksmiths, craftsmen and loggers. Given the imperative to survive, these people have acquired unique knowledge and skills by adapting to the specific constraints and advantages of their fragile, inhospitable

117

environments. They possess millennia of experience in shifting cultivation, terraced fields, and medicinal use of native plants, migratory grazing, and sustainable harvesting of food, fodder, and fuel from forests (Pratap, 2001). With increasing demographic pressure, the failure of the state to protect wildlife (Macleod, 1986; Denniston, 1995), the failure of protected areas to complement their surroundings and recognized the world they fit into (Stem et al, 2003 Daniel et al, 2005; Kruger, 2005), and access to markets there are emerging threats due to unsustainable forest resource use. Can rural peoples derive livelihoods from forests while protecting them? According to Tucker (2000) this question challenges communities for which forests represent a primary resource.

This chapter seeks to identify the forest dependent livelihoods, to assess their impacts on the forest and to appraise the implementation of the community forest management concept in order to identify the scope for designing sustainable strategies and control systems from the perspective of traditional forest management.

The grid reference of the summit of the mountain is $6^0 12`N$, $10^0 23`E$ and Lake Oku $6^0 12`N$, $10^0 27`E$. The northern portion of the mountain is called the Kilum Mountain by Oku villages while the southern portion is called the Ijim or Ejim Mountain by Kom villages. Geographers refer to the mountain as Mount Oku. The forest is found mainly between 2022 and 3011 (summit of the mountia) above sea level. Hawkins and Brunt (1965) describe the climate of the summit as "cool, very cloudy and misty" with maximum temperatures of $16.5^0 c$ to $19^0 c$ and minimum temperatures of $90^0 c$ to $10^0 c$. The rainfall is in excess of 3350mm/ year. The sub-montane area has been described as "cool and misty' with mean maximum temperatures of $20^0 c$ to $22^0 c$ and mean minimum temperatures of $13^0 c$ to $14^0 c$. This rainfall varies from 1780 mm to 2290 mm per year. Most rainfall occurs between July and September. A dry season occurs from mid-October to mid – March (Hollier, 1981).

Geographically the study area is part of the Cameroonian Highlands ecoregion which encompasses the mountains and highland areas of the border region between Nigeria and Cameroon (Stuart, 1986; Gartland, 1989 and Stattersfield et al, 1998). Mount Oku is at an altitude of 3011m above sea level. Most of the area around the mountain is below 2600 m in elevation. The lower boundary of the forest is now determined by conversion to agricultural land. In White's (1983) phytogeographical classification, the area falls within the Afromontane archipelago-like regional centre of endemisms that spans the entire continent.

Macleod (1986) estimates that in 1963, there were approximately 17,500 hectares of forest. By 1986 less than half remained. 33% of the forest was highly degraded (Figure 1). Actual and potential threats causing forest degradation include demographic pressure (72 inhabitants / km^2), grazing, fire damage, a deepening economic crisis at the national level due to the fall in the price of coffee (the main export crop) on the world market and the lack of alternative employment. (Macleod, 1986, Ngwah, 2001).

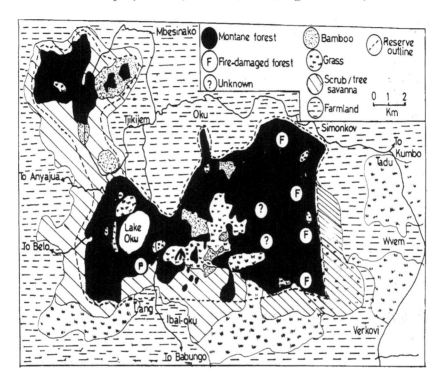

Figure 1: Vegetation derivatives of Kilum-Ijim Mountain Forest: anthropogenic degradation (Situation in 1986 after Macleod).

Jai (2007) and Mbenmbem (2007) also observed that the extraction of timber and non-timber forest products is a major threat due to bad harvesting techniques (unsustainable harvesting of forest products). Between 1983 and 1986 the annual deforestation rate was 567 hectares per year (Macleod, 1986). The retreat of the forest during this period is presented in figure 2.

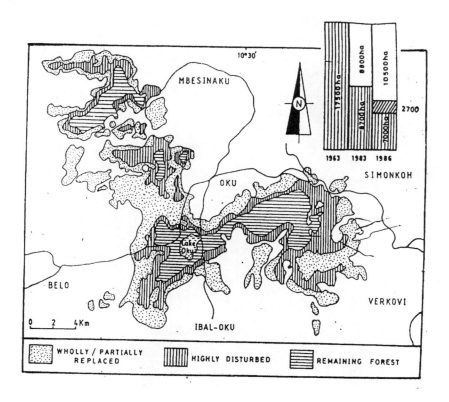

Figure 2: Retreat of Kilum – Ejim forest: Situation at the initiation of the community forestry project in 1986 (Source: Macleod, 1986)

The forests are of great ecological significance. They contain a disjunct vegetation association found nowhere else in West Africa, and several endangered species of plants and animals, including two bird species which are totally dependent on these forests for their survival (Alpert 1993; Garthland 1989; Stuart 1986 and Macleod 1986). The forest provides local employment and livelihood (Ngwah, 2001). Efforts have been made by the national government since the 1930s to protect the forest but these have so far been unsuccessful. Of the forest which occupied the area 50 years ago, less than half remains and at least 33% is highly degraded (Macleod 1986).

Macleod (1986) notes that there have been efforts to declare Oku Mountain forest a reserve since the 1930s. in 1931 it was approved as a forest reserve by the government. In 1985 the reserve status was enforced (Bawden and Langdale –Brown, 1961; Hawkins and Brunt 1965). Partial demarcation of the forest boundary began in 1975 to delimit a zone beyond which farming should not exceed and discourage forest destruction. The demarcation process was never completed and was not adequate. Demarcation pillars were small in size, were disregarded by forest-adjacent villages and so were easily moved. In July 1982, there was a retracing of the 1975 demarcation to find out the extent of encroachment by farming and grazing and the illegal exploitation of forest resources (Figure 1 and 2). In many areas, there had been extensive encroachment and pillars had been uprooted and moved. The area was gazetted a protection forest under the forestry regulation of Cameroon (Law No. 81-13 of 27/11/1981). Within a protection forest, livelihood activities were still allowed to continue provided that they were not in conflict with the conservation of the area and were strictly controlled.

More than 80% of the 300.000 inhabitants derive livelihoods from forest-related activities. Since the 1930s there has been a wide gulf between rhetoric and policy objectives, on the one hand and the reality of policy and project implementation on the other. Numerous environmental laws and regulations remain unenforced, programmes and projects poorly implemented, while measures coined to protect or rehabilitate ecosystems often impinge negatively on livelihoods at the village or local level. (Ndenecho, 2005). In most protected sites technocratic formulae have often been imposed which generally ignore the socio-economic and cultural situation of thousands of families whose livelihoods depend on the forest. This approach has provoked social conflicts which often undermine the possibility of implementing and achieving basic conservation objectives (Gengiz, 2007; Ndenecho, 2007a; Ndenecho, 2007b, Tucker, 2000) Coupled with limited human and financial resources necessary for the administration of protected areas, most reserve status often exist only on paper (Denniston, 1995). The community forest management concept which involves participatory management with local people was adopted in 1995 (Asanga, 1995). Following the promulgation of law No. 94/01 of 20th January 1994, and its decree of application of the 23rd August 1995 the community forestry concept was adopted in the protection of the forest. The local communities co-manage the natural resource base in partnership with the government

Data Sources and Methods

In order to identify the livelihoods dependent on the forest data was obtained using ethnobotanical surveys (Ndenecho, 2006 a; Ndenecho, 2006 b; Duncan, 1989; Thomas, 1986). The survey summarized the useful plant species using their scientific names, local names, plant organs used and the local uses. Based on the work of Ndenecho (2006 b) the useful plants were subsequently classified according to life form, that is, emergent trees, small

121

trees, shrubs, climbers, herbs, epiphytes, succulents, bulbs, corms and tubers. The impact of livelihood activities on the forest was made using a forest damage assessment rating by the Lang Forest user Group (Ngwah, 2001). Sixteen forest user groups under six forest management institutions were identified and mapped (Jai, 2007). The study then conducted a single interview for each community forest management institution using the group leaders. Information was collected in six single interviews on their assessment of the impact of livelihood activities on the forest, the institutionalization of a community forest management strategy and the major constraints involved in its management. The basic hypothesis underlying the group interview is that the group leaders have an excellent "feel" for the community problems and conditions unlike a survey where the respondent is asked to generalize about himself and his livelihoods. In this study the group leaders were asked to generalize about the community and the functioning of user groups.

Results and Discussions

Table 1: Forest user groups (FUG) and institutions in Kilum-Ejim Mountain Forest (Figure 3)

Forest User Groups (FUGs)	Length of Forest Boundary (m)	Forest Management Institution (MFI)
Ngashie	3.332	Emfveh mii
Keyon	1.505	
Manchok	3.296	
Ngvuinkei II	1.295	
Mbockevu	8.466	Upper Shinga
Lang	5.466	
Ngemsiba	1.486	
Ngvuinkei I	4.113	
Mbockenghas	3.860	Nchiiy
Simonkoh	3.139	Mbai
Ichim	3.139	Ijim
Jikijem	2.711	
Mbockejikijem	3.618	
Mboh	2.412	Kejem-mawes
Kesoten	2.982	
Jiyane	3.615	

Source: Jai, 2007

Table 1 and figure 3 present the forest-adjacent villages and the forest management institutions (FMI). A forest management institution is composed of forest user groups (FUG). The area has six FMI and sixteen FUG. The forest management institutions are grouped under an umbrella organisation known as the Association of Forest management Institutions (AFMI). The forest management institutions work with village traditional institutions (Chief, notables, indigenous religious institutions) and related government agencies to design a management plan for the forest. Technical and financial support is rendered by the government of Cameroon through a Technical Operation Unit (TOU) of the Ministry of Forest and the Environment. Between 1986 and 1989 Birdlife International supported the Kilum and Ejim Mountain Forest Projects in the conservation of biodiversity and the promotion of sustainable livelihoods. After 1989 the project facilitated the formation of forest user groups and management institutions. International support ended in 1995 and it was expected that the government will continue to give technical and financial assistance to the villages managing their forest through the Technical Operation Unit.

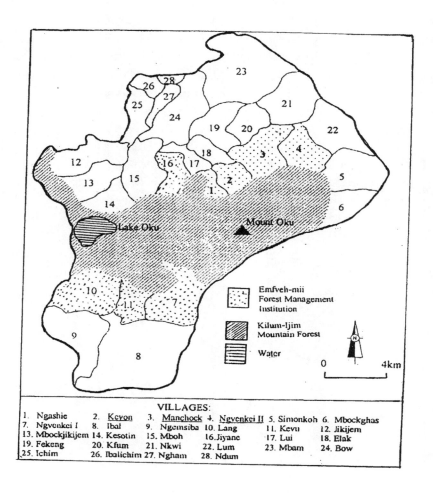

Figure 3: Kilum – Ejim forest –adjacent villages and community forest management institutions (Ndenecho, 2006 a).

The main components of the community forest management plan are decided upon by the user groups in group meetings. These include the objectives and the management rules. The rules guide both the primary and secondary users. The primary users are villagers whose main livelihoods depend on forest products (timber and non-timber forest products). Forest management decisions are made by the primary users. Secondary users are villagers who do not directly depend on the forest. They have grazing and farming rights in designated sites at the forest periphery. Tertiary users are villagers who do not directly use the forest as a source of livelihood. Management plans generally include routine fire-tracing of the forest periphery, routine policing by group members to enforce voluntarily agreed upon rules and regulations, rehabilitation of critically degraded sites and the development and enforcement of land use plans to accommodate the main livelihoods provided by the forest (Table 2).

Table 2: Distribution of plants of Kilum –Ejim forest according to life form, habitat and indigenous uses

Species	Local name	Form	Habitat	Uses
Minulopsis solinsii		HB, SB	FO	FW
AGAVACEAE				
Sanseviera trifasciata	*Elang*	HB, CT	CT	FW
Dracaena deisteliana	*Nkeng*	SB	CT	TR
ALANGIACEAE				
Alaugium Chinese	*Febom*	TL	FO;SC	IN
ANACARDIACEAE				
Sorindeia peleoides	*Kentieh'she*	TS, SB	SC,CT	TR;TC
ARALIACEAE				
Polyscias fulva	*Keghang Kebongsa*	TS;TL	FO;CT	TC;OT
Schefflera abyssinica	*Djia*	TL	FO	TC;HO
Schefflera barteri	*Elang*	TS;EP	FO	FE;MD
Schefflera mannii	*Ebwos-rewus*	T;	FO	TC;HO
APOCYNACEAE				
Rauvolfia vomitoria	*Ebtum*	TS	SC;FO	TC
Tabernaemontana	*Ebtum*	TS	SC;FO	TC
Voacanga Africana	*Ebtum*	TS	FO;CT	MD
BALSAMINACAEAE				
Impatients bartonia	*Kimvas*	HB	SC	FO
BASELLACEAE				
Bassala alba	*Kefu feyin*	LN	SC;FM	MD
BIGNONIA				
Kigelia Africana	*Kinlieh'she*	TS	SC;CT	TR;TC
Markhamia tomentosa	*Enggweh*	TS	SC;CT	MD
BARAGINACEAE				
Cynoglossum	*Imbanen*	HB	SF;FO	MD
Coreopsis barteri	*Foll*	HB	FM;SC	
COMPOSITAE				HO
Crassocephalum manni	*Ngangang*	TS	SC	

125

Emelia coccinea	*Ebjenen*	HB	SC	AG
Vernonia leucocalyx	*Keghanghang*	SB;TS	SC	MD
Vernomia sp.	*Keghanghang*	SB	SC	
CRASSULACEAE				D
Bryophyllum pinnatum	*King-ketuleh*	HB	SC	MD
Kolancchoe lacintiata	*Ketuhleh*	HB	SC	
Kolancchoe laciniata	*Ketuhleh*	HB	SC;FO	MD
CUCURBITACEAE				MD
Momordica foetida	*Ebifierfer Nak*	LH	SC	MD
ERICACEAE				
Aguaria salicifolia	*Bhang*	TS	FO;SC	MD
EUPHORBIACEAE				
Bridelia speciosa	*Eblum*	TS	SC	FE
Croton marcrostacyus	*Ebjam*	TS;TL	FO;SC	TC
Euphorbia kamerunica		HB	CT	MD
Neoboutonia velutina	*Fa'ngum*	TS	FO;SC	MU
Ricinus communis	*Jang*	TS;SB	CT	MD
Sapium ellipticum	*Kehtorh*	TL	FO;SC	MD
FABACEAE				
Phaseolus vulgaris	*Ekuum*	HB	CT	MD
GRAMINAE				
Arundinaria alpina	*Ebtotom*	SB	FO	CF
Melinis minutiflora	*Fejang-e-egwei*	HB	GR	MD
Oxytenanthrea abyssinica	*Mbangsehtotom*	SB	GRLCT	CF
Zea imperata sp.		HB	FM	MD
Leptanlus daphnoides	*Salangang*	TS	FO;GL	DY
LABTATAE				
Plechinthus esculenths	*Ndongfenkeir*	SB	GR;CT;FM	FO
Satureja robusta	*Fegis*	HB	SC	MD
LEEACEAE				
Leea guineensis	*Cheng*	SB	FIMSC	MD
LILIACAEAE				
Albuca nigritata	*Kelend fejin*	SB	GR	MD
MALVACEAE				
Sida rhombifolia	*Nshim*	SB	SC	FB
MARATTIACEAE				
Marattia frazinea	*Kelang*	SB	AQ;FO	MD
MALTACEAE				
Carapa grandiflora	*Evum*	TL	FO	FW

MOSACEAE				
Albizia gummifera	Fuim	TL	FO	TB
Newtonia buchananii	Kilarni	TL	FO	TB
MONIMIACEAE				
Xymalos monospora	Fegei	TS	FO	CF
MORACEAE				
Ficus exasperate	Keghawus	SB	FO	MD
F. oreodryadum	K'ghumfigak	TL	FO	TR;FE
Ficus sp.	Ntoh	TL	FO	FF
MYRSINACEAE	Kenlimlim	LW	FO	FE;MD
Maesa lanceolata	Seim	TS	FO;SC	MD
Rapanea melanoeneura	Ntohkoh	TL	FO	CF
MYRTACEAE				
Syzgium staudtii	Oweh	TL	FO	HO;FN
PALMAE				
Raphia farinifera	Eluk	TS	CT	CF;AL
PAPILLIONACEAE				
Crotalaria	-	SB	SC;FM	AG
Millettia conraui	Efeumen	TS	SB	OT
Sesbania sesban	Eyis	SB	CT;FM	AG
Tephrosia preussii	-	SB	SC;GR	AG
Tephrosia vogelii	Kohlen	SB	CT;FO	AG,MD
PHYTOLACCACEAE				
Phytolacca aodecandra	Etohtam	SB	FO	TR
PIPERACEAE				
Piper capense	Boboi	EPIHB	FO	MD
Piperomia fernadopoisna	Mboi	TS	FO	MD
RHIZOPHORACEAE				
Cossipourea ugandensis	Elung	TL	FO	TB
ROSACEAE				
Prunus africanus	Eblah	TL	FO	MD;TB
Rubus piñata	Bakoh	TF	SC	FO
RUBIACEAE				
Canthium dunlapii	Bangefonembessei	TS	FO	TR
Corynanthe pachyuras	Owing	TL	FO	FW
Curiera longifolia	Ketyelum	TS	FO	FO
RUTACEAE				
Clausena aniseta	Fii	TS	FO	IN;MD

Fagara rubescens	*Bjung*	TS	FO	MU
SAPINDACEA				
Allophyllus bullatus	*Njiabas*	TS	FO	CF
SOLANACEAE				
Datura candida	*Eytohkin*	SB	CT	FE

KEY: * Life form   * Uses (Livelihoods)

TL = large tree =emergent trees   AG= agroforestry
TS=SMALL TREE   FO = food
LN = climber   TB = timber
SB = shrub   AL = alcohol
HB = HERB   FW = firewood
EP = epithyte   TC = wood carving
BB =bulb/tuber/corm   CF=construction fibre
SU = succulent   HO = honey
OT = others

Habitat

IN = insecticide
FO= Forest
GR = grassland   DY= dye
CT = cultivated fields   MU = musical instruments
AQ = aquatic   FE= fence
SC = scrub   MD = medical
FM = farmland   TR = ritual rites/traditional uses.

Table 2 presents the useful plants of Mount Oku and the livelihoods they support (Ndenecho, 2006 a, Ndenecho, 2006 b; Duncan, 1989). It presents the particular use of plant species and the plant organs used. These plants are native to the area. A total of 86 plant species support various livelihood purposes (Ndenecho, 2006 a).

Table 3: Distribution of the useful plants species according to life-form (Ndenecho, 2006 a)

Number of useful plant species per life form								
Users	Large trees	Small trees	Shrubs	Climbers	Epiphytes	Herbs	Bulbs, tubers & corms	Succulents
Timber	5	0	0	0	0	0	0	0
Alcohol	0	1	0	0	0	0	0	0
Firewood	3	0	1	0	0	0	0	0
Wood carving	4	0	1	0	0	0	0	0
Construction	0	5	1	0	0	0	0	0
fibre	3	2	1	0	0	0	0	0
Honey(apicult	1	01	0	0	0	0	0	0
ure)	0	1	0	0	0	0	0	0
Insecticide	0	2	0	0	0	0	0	0
Dye	2	1	4	3	2	11	4	5
Musica	2	9	4	0	0	0	0	0
instrument	0	2	1	0	0	1	0	0
Fencing poles	0	1						
Medicinal								
Agroforestry								
Food								

Large trees = emergent trees.

Photo: Ethnobotanical study in the Oku Mountain Forest Reserve: Forests sustain several local livelihoods.

Photo: Natural pharmacy, the forest at Oku, supplies herbs for healer (insert): traditional healer dependent on the forest, now being studied by ethnobotanists who seek information that might enlarge modern medicine's pharmacopia.

Table 3 analysis the plant life according to life form and uses. The main use categories were timber, alcohol, fuelwood, wood carving, construction wood, fibre, honey, dye, musical instruments, fencing poles, medicinal (remedies, flavourings), insecticides, construction material and agroforestry. Emergent trees, small trees and shrubs offer the highest number of uses. Herbs, bulbs, corms and succulents are mainly used for medicinal purposes. Herbs constitute 27.5%, small trees 22.5%, shrubs 10%, bulbs/corms/tubers 10%, climbers 2%, emergent trees 5 and epiphytes 5% of total medicinal plants. The total number of useful plants are distributed as follows: Medicinal plants 40 species, woodcarving 10 species, agroforestry 6 species, timber 5 species and fire wood 4 species. The rest of the plants offer only minor uses.

Table 4: Damage assessment rating by the Lang Forest User Group

Livelihood	High Damage	Some Damage	No Damage
Hunting		*	
Grazing		*	
Honey (wild)		*	
Honey (hive)		*	*
Carving		*	
Firewood		*	
Trapping		*	
Tool handles	*		
Medicine		*	
Rope			*
Edible fungi			*
Adhesive gum			*
Wild vegetables			*
Traditional red feather			*
Oil containers			*
Agricultural encroachment	*		
Accidental bush fires	*		

Source: Ngwah, 2001

Table 4 presents a forest damage assessment rating per livelihood activity as perceived by the Lang Forest User Group. This is the largest group (Ngwah, 2001). Forest user identified agricultural encroachment, handicraft and accidental bush-fires as major threats to the forest. Hunting, grazing at the forest periphery and invasion of the forest by cattle and goats, wild honey collection resulting in accidental bush-fires, fuelwood collection and the harvesting of medicinal plant organs were judged to be causing some damage to the forest. These according to forest users threatens the sustainability of all livelihoods. From group discussions and informal interviews of forest users, the following constraints in the implementation of the community forest management concept were identified:

- Community environmental knowledge may have accumulated over many generations, but since it is gained from experience it encompasses only those aspects of the local environment which are important to people's livelihoods. Local people tend to have much more comprehensive knowledge of the many uses to which local trees and shrubs may be put, than how actively to grow them.

• Rural livelihoods systems are dynamic. They are open to changes brought about by the primary, secondary and tertiary forest users. Each group applies knowledge in different ways to solve land management problems as they arise. They therefore, show interest in the management of the forest differently. For example, in the event of fighting a devastating forest fire bee keepers react fast because fires will destroy their hives and colonies. Fuel wood gatherers, herbalists, farmers and graziers are apathetic because it does not affect them directly and immediately. This often generates land use conflicts among user groups as the fire will favour some livelihood activities (grazing, farming, fuelwood collection, new growth of herbs and fibres) and will adversely affect other livelihoods (bee keeping, hunting, wood carving).

• The effective adoption and implementation of community forestry is adversely being affected by the process of commodification, that is, the ongoing economic crisis, the lack of alternative livelihood activities and the demand for forest products. This often leads to a sacrifice of the common good for short term individual gain.

• Population pressure on the forest and incipient forest resource depletion in many villages are exceeding the capacity of local institutions to adapt and manage environmental change.

• Interventions of the Technical Operations Unit in community forest management such as the provision of external inputs (material, financial, technical) for the promotion and realization of local potentials have been wanting.

• The process of the participatory mapping and institutionalization of community forests has also been hindered by disputes over land tenure between villages. To resolve these disputes the boundary between the Ejim villages and Kilum villages was demarcated by a plant life sanctuary which today is poorly managed. The process of forest boundary negotiation between villages needs to be facilitated.

• Most importantly, local institutional capacities have been eroded and overwhelmed by the pace of change. The commodification of forest products (penetration of the cash economy) through the Honey Production and Marketing Cooperative, Handicraft Marketing Cooperative and Farmers Cooperatives, fuel wood demands by village bakeries and urban centres, and the commercial and industrial exploitation of Pygeum africanus bark have caused the poor and powerless to local access to productive resources as powerful local interest groups, individuals and outsiders consolidate their control over them. This has led to resource "mining" of forests and natural pastures. The forest management institutions are therefore fragile due to the weakening of community controls and stability.

The forest management institutions charged with the conservation of their local forests deriving livelihoods from them and exhorted to plant trees in critically degraded sites are failing to achieve these objectives. The community management scheme lacks both the real backing of the primary, secondary and tertiary users (local people) and the institutional means to make enforcement effective. Due to this failure land degradation is continuing (Jai, 2007; Mbenmbem, 2007; Icick, 2007,; Bekolo, 2001). Arnold and Campbell (1985) recommended that community sanctions are the ideal mechanism for the enforcement of rights through voluntary agreements of rights in fairly small and clearly defined village groups. They argue that this approach is more likely to put local people's priorities first, to be effective and to be sustainable in economic and social terms. Table 5 summarizes the many types of possible control systems which can be used in traditional management by villages.

Table 5: Distribution of control systems in traditional forest management by illustration of uses

	Basis of group rules	Examples
	Harvesting only selected components	• Trees: timber, fuelwood, fruit, nuts, seeds, honey, leaf fooder, fibre, life mulch, other minor products (gums, resins, dyes, liquor, plated leaves, etc) • Grass: fodder, thatching, rope, • Other wild plants: medicinal herbs, food, bamboos, etc. • Other cultivated plants: maize, millet, wheat, potatoes, beans, vegetables, fruits, etc. • Wildlife: animals, birds, bees, other insects, etc.
	Harvesting according to condition of products	• Stage of growth: maturity, alive or dead • Size, shape • Plant density, spacing • Season (flowering, leaves fallen, etc) • Part: branch, stem, shoot, flower.
	Limiting amount of product	• By time: season, days, year, several years • By quantity: of trees, head loads, baskets,

		animals
		• By tools: sickles, saws, axes, hoes, cutlasses
		• By area: Zoning, block, types of terrain, altitude
		• By agency: women, hired labour, children, contractor, type of animal.
	Using social means for protecting areas	• By watcher: paid in grains or cash • By rotational guard duty • By voluntary group action • By making mandatory the use of herders to watch animals

Source: Modified after Arnold and Campbell (1985)

The critical issue is not so much what rules are applied but the strength of community institutions which set the rules and ensure that they remain effective. Community sanctions are most likely to arise spontaneously and work where a cohesive social and administrative structure exists. This will tend to be in relatively isolated villages which are little affected by commodification and rapidly changing socio-economic framework conditions. There is a need to search for ways of strengthening the basis for the enforcement of management regulations in the villages. It may be possible to support and strengthen existing structures and institutions, or create new ones where the basis of rule making is totally lacking.

Conclusion and Recommendations

The "conservationist" approach to biodiversity conservation has failed to come to grips with crucial social issues – it ignores the socio-economic and cultural situation of rural people whose livelihoods depend on the forest. It provokes conflicts which often undermine the possibility of implementing and achieving basic conservation objectives. There is need to search for new forest management models. The community management model can enhance the sustainable development of forest-adjacent communities if the following crucial aspects are considered.

• Access right must be transferred to fairly small and dearly defined user groups through voluntary agreement of use rights.

• Forest exploitation and communities empowered to undertake sustainable harvesting of products.

- Local institutions must be supported and strengthened as a base for the enforcement control systems, rule making, provision of environmental education, supervision, organisation and use of resources and to ensure a fair distribution of income.
- The establishment of a control and functioning mechanism as a prerequisite for achieving ecological stability
- The setting up of large conservancies at village level with user groups that will monitor access, set quotas and control access.
- Promotion of conservation initiatives at the level of forest user groups based on sustainable management and self-financing. Current financing through international aid and state funding has failed.

References

Alpert, P. (1993) Conserving biodiversity in Cameroon. *Ambio*. No 22, p. 33-107

Asanga, C, (1995) Community forestry in Cameroon. KMFP Report, Elak-Oku.12p.

Bekolo, A, (2001) Foresterie Communautaire au Cameroun: Processus, constraints, Perspective. *Proceedings of National Sensitization Workshop on Ecofarming in Cameroon: December 10th to 11th , Bamenda*, p. 73-80

Bawden, M. and Langdale – Brown, I. (1961) An aerial photograph reconnaissance of the present and possible land uses in Bamenda area, Directorate of overseas Studies, London. 25p.

Arnold, J and Campbell, J. (1985) Collective management of hill forest in Nepal: Community forestry Project. Washington D.C National Academy of Science.

Daniel, L.; Manning, R.; Krymkowski, D. (2005) the relationship between visitor-based standards of quality and existing conditions in parks and outdoor recreation. *Leisure Sciences*, Vol. 27. p. 157-73.

Denniston, D. (1995) Sustaining mountain peoples and environments. World-Watch Institute Report on Progress Towards a Sustainable Society. W.W. Norton and Campany, London. p. 38-57.

Duncan, T. (1989) La conservation des ecosystems forestiers du cameroun. IUCN, Gland and Cambridge.

Gengiz, T. (2007) Tourism, an ecological approach in protected areas: karagol-Sahara National Park, Turkey. The Inter. Journal of Sustainable Development and World Ecology. Vol. 14.No. 3. p. 260-67.

Hawkins, P. and Brunt, M. (1965) Soils and ecology of West Cameroon. FAO Report No. 2083, Rome, p. 162-171.

Hollier, G. (1981) The dynamics of rural Marketing in North West Province, Cameroon, Unpublished PhD Thesis, Department of Geography, University of Liverpool. 212 p.

Ichick, M. (2007) Sustaining rural livelihoods in Oku village. Unpublished Long Essay, Deparment of Geography (ENS), University of Yaounde 1. 36 p.

Jai, J. (2007) Forest user groups and community forest mapping in Kilum Mountain forest, Unpublished Long Essay, Department of Geography (ENS), University of Yaounde I, 30 p.

Kruger, O. (2005) The role of ecotourism in conservation. *Biodiversity and conservation*, Vol. 14, p. 579-600.

Macleod, H. (1986) The conservation of Oku Mountain Forest, Cameroon. ICBP Project Report, Cambridge 90 p.

Mbenmbem, Y. (2007) Sustaining rural livelihoods in mountain ecosystems: Case study of Oku. Unpublished Long Essay, Department of Geography (ENS), University of Yaounde I. 35 p.

Ndenecho, E. (2005) Conserving biodiversity in Africa: Wildlife management in Cameroon. *Loyola Journal of Social Sciences*, Vol. 19, No. 2. p. 209-228.

Ndenecho, E. (2006 a) Habitat loss and the survival of endemic montane forest avifauna of Bamenda Highlands, Cameroon. *Journal of Environmental Sciences*, Vol. 10, No. 1, p. 1-16.

Ndenecho, E. (200 a) Degradation of useful plants in Oku tropical montane cloud forest, Cameroon *International Journal of Biodiversity Science and Management,* Vol. 2, No. 2. p. 75-86.

Ndenecho, E. (2006 b) Ethnobotanical survey of Oku montane cloud forest, Cameroon *Journal of environmental Sciences* Vol. 10, No. 2 p. 13-29.

Ndenecho, E. (2007 b) Population dynamics, rural livelihoods and forest protection projects in Sub-Saharan Africa; experiences from Santa, Cameroon. *International Journal of Sustainable Development and World Ecology,* Vol. 14, No. 3. p. 250-259.

Pratap, T. (2001) Mountain agriculture, marginal lands and sustainable livelihoods: Challenges and opportunities. *International Symposium on Mountain Agriculture in HKH region, 21-24 May,* 1984, ICIMOD, Kathmandu.

Roy, W. (2001) Global viewpoint on mountains. In: J. Dunlop and W. Roy (eds.), Culture and environment. University of Buea/ University of Strachlyde. p. 113-136.

Statterfield, A; Crosby, J.; Long. J; and Wege, D. (1998) Endemic bird areas of the world: priorities for biodiversity conservation. Birdlife Conservation Series, No. 7 Bird life Internaitonal Cambridge. p. 3-17.

Stem. C.; Lassoie, J.; Lee, D.; Deshler, D.; and Schelhas J. (2003) Community participation in ecotourism benefits; the link to conservation practices and perspectives. *Society and Natural Resources,* Vol. 16, p. 387-413.

Stuart, S.N. (1986) Conservation of Cameroon montane forests. Report of the ICBP Cameroon Montane forest Survey, Cambridge.

Thomas, W.D. (1986) Vegetation in the Montane Forests of Cameroon, International Council for Bird Preservation, Cambridge.

Tucker, C (2000) Striving for sustainable forest management in Mexico and Honduras: the experience of two communities. In: *Mountain Research and Development,* Berne-Switzerland, vol. 20, p. 116-117.

White, F. (1983) The vegetation of Africa, UNESCO/AETFAT/ UNSO Vegetation Map of Africa 1:5000.000 UNESCO, Paris, 3 plates.

Chapter 8

Gender Roles and Power Relationships in Environmental Protection

Case Study: Agro-forestry programme of the Bamenda Highlands

Summary

Divisions between men and women in access to natural resources and in their management and use are common in African land management systems. Women constitute the bulk of small-scale resource-limited farmers. Yet, cropland is often not directly under their control. It is usually controlled either by their husbands, brothers or fathers. Therefore, both tenure and gender considerations necessarily go together. The chapter examines gender relations and land tenure as they affect the development of agroforestry using a combination of primary and secondary data sources. The study collates data on land tenure, age and sex characteristics of farm households, farm size and access to land, gender division of labour and farm family labour input in order to establish the gender sensitive issues in agroforestry development. It concludes that agroforestry practices can alleviate some of the burdens of women. Yet, land tenure issues as they affect agroforestry development do not favour women. The chapter therefore advocates gender targeted strategies that deliberately integrate both men and women farmers in agroforestry development with the broader context of a farming systems development paradigm. In examining land tenure issues as they affect the development of agroforestry, it is important to recognize that both tenure and gender considerations go together.

Key Words: Land tenure, gender division of labour, land degradation, land management, farming system development, agroforestry development, gender sensitive, gender targeting.

Introduction

A large literature has documented the important role of women in agriculture and food production (Jackson, 1994) and many micro studies of time use have shown the differences in male and female time inputs to crop husbandary (Mueller, 1984; Henn, 1978). Jackson (1994) reviews studies which have demonstrated the significance of equity issues in the process of

139

environmental management and degradation. These have shown that the poor are most negatively affected by environmental degradation (Jodha, 1986), that the poor are often blamed for resource degradation (Drinkwater, 1989), that resource degradation is often related to processes of accumulation, social differentiation and commercialization (Blaikie and Brookfield, 1987; Cliffe and Moorson, 1979), and that poverty drives rural people to exploit the environment (Blaikie, 1986). Class analyses of the causes and consequences of environmental degradation consider only one aspect of equity. Jackson (1994) argues that environmental degradation is a gendered process and we need to view environmental change through the lens of gender relations. The insight derived from gender analysis have contributed to a general paradigm shift in social sciences in which the relativity of actors perceptions has become clear – the environment is perceived by rural women and rural men differently and assumptions underlying early thinking on women and the environment are now being challenged (IDS Policy Briefly – Issue No. 5):

- The assumption that participation in projects will of itself ensure that women will gain when in reality it depends on the type of participation and terms on which it takes place;
- The tendency to treat women as a homogeneous group, ignoring the important differences between them and;
- The simplistic assumption that women's interests and those of the environment are necessarily the same.

Division of labour between men and women in access to natural resources, and in their management and use, are common in African land use management systems. Concerning land tenure and rights there is the crucial issue of women's rights to land and trees and hence to fuelwood (William, 1985). The widespread practice of bush burning in farming systems in Africa is a frequent target of education campaigns because to the outsider it appears to be destructive. Men and women have different reasons for bush burning. Whereas men may burn to ease clearing, women often burn to stimulate a nitrogen flush for crops and to stimulate the fruit and nut production of trees (William, 1985). Environmental degradation will therefore have impacts on men and women gender division of labour. Gender land use concerns and targeting as used in this study refers to the formal and informal policies that are taken to address some of the men's and women's issues related to land tenure and agroforestry development.

Women constitute the bulk of small-scale resource-limited farmers in the Bamenda Highlands. However, cropland is often not directly under their control, it is usually controlled, by either their husbands, brothers or fathers

(Vabi, 1994). Therefore, both tenure and gender considerations necessarily go together. The chapter examines gender relations in the maize-based farming system and land tenures as they affect the development of agroforestry (a current buzz-word of development forestry, natural resource management and rural development) in sub-Saharan Africa.

The area is characterized by soaring mountain peaks, valleys, plains, plateaus and escarpments with an altitudinal range of 1100 to 3010m above sea level. The submontane zone is characterized by cold, cloudy and misty weather (1800 to 2500m) while the areas below 1800m elevation are humid and hot. The rainy season starts in Mid-March and ends in Mid-November. The rest of the year is the dry season. Annual average temperature is about 20^0c. it must be noted that temperature however varies with elevation. Vegetation characteristics form a mosaic of cultivated fields, fallows, natural pastures of savannah and savannah woodlands, gallery forests and remnants of montane and submontane evergreen forests refuged in remote escarpments, mountain valleys and peaks (Letouzey, 1979). This anthropic landscape is the result of centuries of intensive degradation of montane and submontane forests (Tamura, 1986; Hawkins and Brunt 1965; Nkwi and Warnier, 1982). Average population density is about 96 inhabitants per square kilometer. The soils are ultosols; poor in major nutrients, acidic and have high phosphorus requirements (Yamoah et al. 1994). Furthermore, some food crop fields are found on steep slopes where erosional losses are phenomenal as is decline in soil fertility. These soils are derived from basalts, trachytes and granites. These rocks present surface water yields with marked seasonality of flow. Using purchased inputs to overcome the above land degradation scenarios in the traditional farming setting appears remote because farmers lack adequate cash and good input delivery network.

For generations farmers have recognized the role of indigenous trees as soul improvers and this has led to the emergence of the compound farm system with outlying bush fallow fields. The compound farms have coffee as the main crop and are the enterprise of the men while the outlying fields have maize as the main crop and are managed by women. Over the past three decades research and extension efforts have been focused on the integration of agroforestry in the traditional crop production systems.

The Bamenda Highlands constitute a unique geomorphological unit which coincides with the administrative unit known as the North West Province of Cameroon. According to a UNDP/MINPAT report (1999) the area is predominantly rural, with 86% of the poor living in rural areas, and nearly two in three rural residents classed as poor. In terms of regional disparities, the 1996 household survey by the Ministry of Economy and Finance notes that a significant percentage of the poor live in the Northern

Provinces of the country. The North West Province is ranked third out of the ten provinces with an estimation of 365,352 poor (Fonchingong, 2004). The World Bank report (1999) further notes that Women constitute 52% of the three million poor who cannot afford even the food components of a "consumption basket". This indicates a situation of extreme poverty (The World Bank, 1995). In Cameroon, women make up the majority of the poor trapped below the poverty line and poverty is particularly acute for women living in rural areas and heading households (UNDP, 1998).

Poverty is rife in the study area as a result of high population density (over 96 inhabitants / km^2), ruggedness of the terrain, remoteness from markets, the drudgery of transportation, isolation and the fragility of mountain environments. The North West Provincial Service of Statistics (1999) estimates an average farm family size of 10.2 persons, with the largest households having 13.2 persons. Most farm family heads (82%) are married and predominantly male (81%). In terms of literacy, 24% had no schooling, 54% primary 1 to 7 and 14% some secondary education. In rural areas 89% of households send children to school, that is 71% of school age children from farming households attend school. As the foregoing suggests, the level of professional training in agriculture and general education in farm families is negligible. The Provincial Service of statistics estimates it to be 2% and concludes that this notwithstanding, in 14% of farm households the literacy level was:

- 12% of male farm family heads received informal training in agriculture;
- 2% of female farm family heads received informed training in agriculture provided by various non-governmental organizations and the Agricultural Extension Service of the Ministry of Agriculture.

Agriculture is the backbone of the study area. A survey by the Provincial Service of Statistics (1999) indicated the following sources of farm family income: crop cultivation (90.8% of the farm families), livestock raising (52.5% of the farm families), fisheries (5.4% of the farm families), forestry (19.6% of the farm families), apiculture (16.2% of the farm families) and palm wine tapping (28.1% of the farm families). According to Fonchingong (2004) women constitute approximately 54% and men 46% of the economically active population.

There has been deepening rural poverty in the study area since the mid 1980s due to the prevailing economic crisis. Rural women therefore constitute the most vulnerable group. The World Bank (1989) lists the ways in which women are disadvantaged. These include access to land rights, credit, technology, extension services and to education. Since women constitute the largest proportion of the rural poor and the largest proportion of the farming population, they are central in any efforts in reducing poverty. Gender targeting in land management should be central in development efforts because women as land users abuse the land and are therefore victims of environmental degradation. Gender concerns and targeting as employed in this study refers to policies to address women's concerns in sustainable land use development and farm labour deployment.

Data Sources and Methods

The study used the 1972/73 and the 1989/90 Agricultural census results of the Ministry of Agriculture to establish the land tenure classification and the age and sex distribution of the farm household population respectively. Base maps, aerial photographs and archival material of the Provincial Service of Statistics were used to generate data on land use intensity, farm size and related gender sensitive issues. The farm family gender division of labour and labour input per crop cycle was established based on the work of McHughe (1987) in Mezam and Ngoketunjia areas of the Bamenda Highlands. The data so obtained was used together with open ended questions to assess the gender sensitive issues in agroforestry development and the strategic gender needs of women and men in the promotion of this technology. Informal interviews of both male and female farm household yielded data on the complex land tenure issues affecting gender and tree planting. These were complemented by secondary data sources.

Data Analysis and Discussion

Table 1: Land tenure classification in the Bamenda Highlands

Land Tenure Class	Land Area	
	Hectares	Percentage
Title land	1,332	1.0
Money rent	1,256	0.9
Share cropping	1,206	0.9
Mixed rent: money and share cropping	613	0.5
Temporary lease on rental basis	14,047	10.4
Permanent land under lineage control	105,900	78.6
Temporary land under lineage control	8,691	6.4
Squatter	1,754	1.3
Total	138,801	100

Source: 1972/73 Agricultural census, p. 207. Ministry of Agriculture.

Table 1 breaks down the way in which land is controlled into eight categories. An insignificant amount of land is held as private or titled property (1.0%). In general a large proportion of land is still under lineage control. The procedures for obtaining land titles are long and complicated and together with the traditional land allocation institutions exclude women from obtaining titled land in rural areas (Vobi, 1994). Prevailing socio-cultural practices exclude women from land inheritance and also from the position of heirs. Women's rights to land are therefore derived from men, husbands, brothers, uncles and fathers. Similarly control over land and trees are held by men. Direct access to land is difficult for female farm family heads who must obtain land through share cropping, money rent and squatter. Women are therefore under-represented in decision-making related to land distribution and control despite the fact that they contribute the highest labour input to food crop cultivation (Tables 2 and 4). Table 1 highlights the main institutional problems affecting agroforestry development:

- The prevalence of too many land allocation institutions; and

- The inability of women to obtain titled land property due to the land inheritance system that favours males, and the long and complicated procedures for obtaining land titles from the government; and

- The planting of perennial crops and economic trees on leased land often conflicts with the customary land allocation institutions. The right to trees belongs to men. Consequently, without any clear tenure arrangements, women are confronted with a climate of uncertainly over the continued use of land in permanent crops such as trees and other perennial plants.

There is need to simplify existing land allocation procedures to recognize the rights of women to trees and land and dialogue to sensitize local institutions on land allocation matters. Deliberate efforts must therefore be made to give women access to resources that enhance sustainable or permanent farming systems based on indigenous knowledge systems. Agroforestry is one of these resource management technologies. Female farmers are generally given land and told what to plant on it. Tree planting is out of the question because trees guarantee the right of land ownership under customary land tenure systems.

Table 2: The age and sex distribution of farm family population in the Bamenda Highlands

Age (years)	< 5 years	5 – 14 years	15 – 34 years	35 – 64 years	> 64 years	Total
Female	64,060	137,070	136,630	83,820	6,340	427,920
Male	77,800	137,310	68,750	73,540	10,190	367,530
Total	141,860	274,380	205,380	157,360	16,530	795,500
% Female	45.15	49.95	66 .50	56.44	38.35	53.79
% Male	54.85	50.04	33.50	43.56	61.65	46.21

Source: Ministry of Agriculture: 1989 Agricultural survey.

Table 2 presents the age and sex distribution of the farm family population. Children less than 14 years of age have more males, that is, 54.8% for those less than 5years and 50% for those between 5 and 14 years. Females between 15 and 34 years constitute 66.5% of the farm family household population, and 56.4% of the household population between the ages 35 to 64 years. Above 64 years men constitute about 38% of the farm family population. Women and men constitute approximately 54% and 46% of the farm household population respectively. A survey of households by the Provincial Service of Statistics shows a poverty rate of 52.5% with women constituting the majority (Fonchingong, 2004). This is because of the high population density, infertile soils, ruggedness of the land, and inaccessibility to markets, and a rural economy that thrives on subsistence agriculture. Market-oriented farming is found mainly in areas with dense cultivation, that is, where the population density is greater than 100 inhabitants/km2 (See Figure 1). Productive land is limited. As shown in figure 1, if sufficient crop, animal protein and forest products, are to be produced, competition for land is to be expected. This is especially true given the high population density. Land degradation will therefore adversely affect women who constitute the bulk of the farm family population. Scott (1980) notes that the average farm size ranges from 0.5 to 10 hectares and that the farm size distribution is relatively skewed. Farms less than 1.5 hectares (72.7%) account for over 43.3% of the cultivated land. The average size of holding is 2.5 hectares with variations from less than 1 hectare to 10 hectares. Holdings are commonly fragmented with an average plot size of 0.9 hectares.

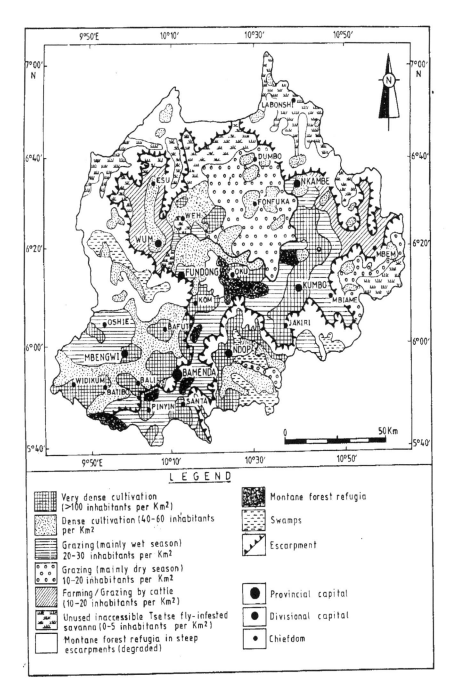

Figure 1: Land use intensity in the North West Province of Cameroon.

Table 3: The age and sex distribution of farm family heads in the Bamenda Highlands.

Age (years)	Total Population	Male family heads		Female family heads	
		No.	%	No.	%
> 25	4,060	4,060	100.0	0	0.0
25 – 34	22,570	19,870	88.0	2,700	12.0
35 – 44	27,540	21,890	79.5	5,650	20.5
45 – 64	63,560	46,870	73.7	16,690	26.3
< 65	10,140	8,840	87.2	1,300	12.8
Total	127,870	101,530	79.4	26,340	20.6

Source: Ministry of Agriculture: 1989 Agriculture Census.

Table 3 presents the age and sex distribution of farm family heads. Women and men constitute 20.6% and 79.4% of farm family heads respectively. There are no female farm family heads below 25 years of age. All farm family heads in this age group are male. This certainly reflects the land inheritance systems which give access to land only to males. This is also reflected in the following age groups: 25 to 34 years (88%), 35 to 44 years (79.5%), 45 to 64 years (73.7%) and above 65 years (87.2%). Despite their being a majority in the farm family household population (53.8%) women have no access to land acquisition by inheritance and so most women are landless or marginalized. Women have access to land through their husbands and other male relatives. Female household heads can only obtain temporary use rights from relatives or short duration of land use rights. Under these circumstances tree planting is not feasible. Male farm family heads as it concerns tree planting for agroforestry are ignorant. Yet, the right to plant trees belongs to men under the customary system.

Table 4: Gender division of labour in a maize-based farming system based on a six-hour work day in the Bamenda Highlands

Table 4a: Total labour input by labour class per crop cycle

Labour class	Man hours/hectare	Percentage
Wife	860.2	46.8
Husband	316.1	17.2
Children (male + female)	261.0	14.2
Farm group (female)	169.1	9.2
Hired labour (male + female)	91.9	5.0
Others (male + female)	139.7	7.6
Total	**1838**	**100**

Table 4b: Land preparation and planting labour input per labour class per crop cycle

Labour class	Man hours/hectare	Percentage
Wife	419.9	48.6
Husband	157.2	18.2
Children (male + female)	96.8	11.2
Farm group (female)	36.3	4.2
Hired labour (male + female)	97.6	11.3
Other (male + female)	56.2	6.5
Total	**864**	**100**

Table 4c: Weeding labour input per labour class per crop cycle

Labour class	Man hours/hectare	Percentage
Wife	285.3	55.4
Husband	73.1	14.2
Children (female)	77.3	15.0
Farm group (female)	22.1	4.3
Hired labour (female)	18.6	3.6
Others (female)	38.6	7.5
Total	**515**	**100**

Table 4d: Labour input for harvesting per labour class per crop cycle

Labour class	Man hours/hectare	Percentage
Wife	154.3	44.2
Husband	49.9	14.3
Children (male + female)	93.9	26.9
Farm group (female)	10.5	3.0
Hired labour (male)	9.8	2.8
Others (male)	30.6	8.8
Total	**349**	**100**

Source, McHughe, 1987.

Table 4a presents the total labour input by labour class. Women provided 46.8% of the total crop cycle labour requirements per hectare while the men provided less than half the labour input of women (17.2%). The labour input of children was almost comparable to that of men (14.2%). Farm groups contributed 9.2% of the labour requirements. It should be noted that these groups are almost totally constituted by women. One can therefore safely conclude that women contribute about 56% of the farm family labour requirements. Most of the hired labour and uncosted labour from the extended family is also dominated by women. Children between 5 and 14 years of age help out with most tasks, especially during the peaks in labour requirements. It is at these times that labour is hired. Table 4b, 4c and 4d present the gender division of labour by farm operation. Labour requirements for bush clearing, soil tillage and planting were established at 864 man hours per hectare or 74% of total labour requirements. Women contributed 48.6%, while the men contributed only 18.2% and children 11.2%. Men's labour input accounted for less than half the labour input of women. (Table 4c). Weeding is one of the most labour demanding farm operations taking up about 28% (515 man hours) of the total labour requirements. Table 4c shows that women contribute 55.4% of the labour required for weeding while the men only 14.2%. Children 26.9% and husbands 14.3%. Wives contributed almost four times the input of the husbands while the children contributed about two times the input of the husbands. It must also be noted that the labour class considered as children is dominated by girls. Weeding and harvesting are farm operations largely handled by wives and female children.

Table 2 establishes that women constitute an important proportion of the crop farming population while table 4 establishes that the bulk of the farm operations are undertaken by them. As such they are most affected by the problems of decreasing soil fertility and shortages of tree products. Agroforestry development can make a contribution to boost or at least maintain current levels of crop production if those involved in the development of agroforestry technologies focus on gender issues in order to formulate targeted policies that deliberately integrate male and female farmers in the design of agroforestry development strategies.

Table 5: Gender sensitive issues in agroforestry development. (Sample size = 135)

No	Gender Sensitive issues in agroforestry as perceived by women	Respondents	Percentage
1	Perception of tree planting by men as an eventual step towards land ownership	135	100.0
2	Inadequate land security for women	73	54.1
3	Short duration of land rights	78	57.8
4	Women have less access to land than men	135	100.0
5	Few female technical staff as extension workers	135	100.0
6	Tree planting seen as the traditional role of men	135	100.0
7	Traditionally defined roles of women limit their participation in agroforestry	112	89.6
8	Undeclared intention of land use to landlord (No decision-making on land use)	79	58.5
9	Women as main land users do not have land titles	126	93.3
10	Women have little technical information on agroforestry	129	95.6
11	Women do not have enough cash to buy farmland	135	100.0

Table 5 presents gender sensitive issues in agroforestry as perceived by female farmers. These are constraints to the development of agroforestry and require that agroforestry promoters integrate gender concerns in development programmes. Development strategies must recognize the complex interdependences between men and women. Within this framework it is necessary to understand the land tenure system and the related gender issues because men and women have differential assets, access to production assets and opportunities. Gender targeting in outreach activities therefore becomes an important aspect of development programmes which must handle the strategic gender needs for men and women.

Table 6: Percentage distribution of domestic tasks by sex in the farm family

Domestic task	Wife		Husband	
	No	%	No	%
Food preparation (cooking)	94	94%	7	7%
House cleaning	96	96%	4	4%
Fetching firewood	100	100%	10	10%
Fetching water	93	93%	5	5%
Washing of clothes	95	95%	4	4%
Child care	95	95%	3	3%

Note: Percentage computed from a sample of 100.

Table 6 presents the distribution of tasks by sex and domestic activity in a sample of 100 farm family households. Women have a disproportionate share of the household economy. Women bear and socialize children, keep the home, fetch firewood and water. Ekwoge (1994) estimates that together with food crop cultivation women put in 14 to 18 hours of work in various tasks per day. Ekwoge concludes that agroforestry practices can uplift some of these burdens of women, that is save time which would have been used to travel long distances in search of fertile land to cultivate, to fetch firewood, water and other timber and non-timber products. Also, continuously working a piece of land reduces land preparation processes which save labour. The time and labour saved by adopting agroforestry practices can be used to do domestic tasks.

Conclusions and Implications

Gender aspects play an important role in societies still oriented to traditional village rule. As such they also influence land management. Women as producers of food prepare the soil, seed, plant, weed and harvest in a cycle which spans season after season. As a matter of fact, they carry out an enormous task to keep the soil fertile and maintain and even improve the harvest, as the families are growing continuously. The advantages of agroforestry development for women include:

- Time-saving: Women do not need to travel long distances to fetch wood, water and to look for fertile land. Time saved can be used for other things;
- Shade provision: Women enjoy a good shade when toiling in the field and resting. A good shade also protects little children;
- Income generation: Fruit trees and spices can augment farm family incomes;
- Soil improvement: Trees play a vital role in soil improvement. Women can use a piece of land continuously and do not spend money on chemical fertilizers;
- Soil conservation: Apart from maintaining soil fertility trees improve the soil structure through the addition of organic matter, increased soil moisture content, and soil erosion control;
- Constant and good quality water supply since women are those who fetch water for domestic use;
- Provision of useful products: Women do not need to walk along distance to harvest useful tree organs (medicines, spices, fuelwood);
- Labour saving: Time saved in walking over long distances and in continuously tilling a piece of land saves labour; and
- Land management: By practicing agroforestry, the little pieces of land women have can be used continuously.

Yet, land tenure issues as they affect agroforestry development do not favour women. Generally, most women like to practice agroforestry when introduced to the concept. However, they still have the constraint of access to permanent land. For women to benefit substantially from the above advantages interventions should seek to integrate gender issues within the context of a farming system development paradigm. If not, tenure will remain an important constraint to the development of agroforestry as a viable land management strategy in societies with traditional rule.

Refernces

Blaikie, P. (1985) The political economy of soil erosion in developing countries. Longman, London.

Blaikie, P. and Brookfield, H. (1987) Land degradation and society. Metheun, London.

Cliffe, L. and Moorson, R. (1979) Rural class formation and ecological collapse in Botswana. Review of African Political Economy, Vol. 14-16, London.

Drinkwater, M. (1989) Technical development and peasant improvement: Land use policy in Zimbabwe's Midlands Province. Journal of Southern African Studies, vol. 15, No. 2.

Ekwoge, G. (1994) Agroforestry and Women. In: Proceedings of Agroforestry Harmonization Workshop. 4th -7th April, 1994, Regional College of Agriculture Bambili, Bamenda.

Fonchingong, C. (2004) Integrating gender concerns for livelihood improvement and local development in North West Cameron: The case of NGOs. In: Journal of Applied Social   Sciences, University of Buea.

Hawkins, P. and Brunt, M. (1965) Soils and ecology of West Cameroon. F.A.O Rome.

Henn, J. (1978) Peasant workers and capital: the political economy of labour and incomes in Cameroon. Unpublished Ph. D Thesis. Harvard University, Massachusetts.

IDS (1995) New thinking on gender and the environment. IDS Policy Briefing – Issues 5. Institute of Development Studies, Sussex. p. 1-4

Jackson, C. (1994) Environmental reproduction and gender relations. Journal of the Society for International Development. Vol. 1 p. 72-75.

Letouzey, R. (1979) Vegetation, In: Atlas of the United Republic of Cameroon. Editions Jeune Afrique, Paris. P. 20-24.

McHughe, D. (1987) Maize-based farming systems in Ndop Plain, North West Province – Cameroon. USAID/IITA/IRA Bambui.

Mueller, E. (1984) The value and allocation of time in rural Botswana. Journal of Development Economics. Vol. 15 No. 1. pp. 329-360.

Nkwi, P. N. and Warnier, J-P. (1982) Elements for a history of the Western Grassfields. Publication of Department of Sociology, University of Yaounde.

Provincial Service of Statistics (1999) Baseline Survey of the rural world situation in the North West Province of Cameroon. Provincial service of Statistics NWP, Bamenda.

Scott, W. (1980) Development in the Western Highlands, United Republic of Cameroon. USAID/Cameroon, Yaounde.

Tamura, T. (1986) Regolith stratigraphic study of Late Quaternary environmental history in West Cameroon Highlands and the Adamawa Plateau. In: H. Kadomura (ed.) Geomorphology and environmental changes in tropical Africa: Case Studies in Cameroon and Kenya. Hokkaido University. Pp. 83-90.

The World Bank (1995) Cameroon: Poverty assessment. The World Bank, Washington D.C.

The World Bank (1989) Sub-Saharan Africa: From crisis to sustainable growth – long-term perspective study. The World Bank, Washington D. C.

The World Bank (1999) A 1999 update of the Cameroon poverty profile. The World Bank office, Yaounde – Cameroon.

UNDP (1988) Integrating human rights with sustainable development. A UNDP policy document, UNDP, New York.

UNDP/MINPAT (1999) Regional socio-economic study of Cameroon. The North West Province Project, UNDP office, Yaounde.

Yamoah, C.; Ngueguim, M.; Ngong, C. and Cherry, S. (1994) Soil fertility conservation for sustainable crop production: Experiences from some highlands areas of North West Province. In: Proceedings of Agroforestry Harmonisation Workshop. GTZ, USAID, and Helvetas, RCA Bambili. p. 1-6.

William, P. W. (1985) Women and forestry, special invited paper for the ninth World Forestry Congress. Mexico City.

Vabi, M. (1994) Land tenure and potential for agroforestry development in North West Province of Cameroon. Proceedings of Agroforestry Harmonization Workshop, 4th to 7th April, 1994, Regional College of Agriculture Bambili, Bamenda.

Chapter 9

Ecological Planning and Ecotourism Development in Protected Areas

Case Study: Kimbi Game Reserve

Summary

Game reserves and other protected areas are potential areas for the development of ecotourism because of their biodiversity, landscapes and cultural heritage of local or indigenous people. This study investigates the environmental sustainability of game reserves using a sample of the Kimbi Game Reserve. It assesses the potentials of the reserve for the development of ecotourism by employing a combination of field observation, examination, data collection and evaluation, using a SWOT analysis. The SWOT analysis determines opportunities and threats, and strategic suggestions for ecological planning. The study determines usage potential and the types of ecotourism feasible for development, and appraises the current management strategies. It concludes that ill-adapted strategies are bound to fail in promoting ecotourism, attaining sustainable landscapes and livelihoods. The Kimbi Game Reserve has economic potential for ecotourism which can be realized by integrating the cultural values, livelihoods and environmental awareness of local people in tourism development. Finally, the chapter recommends that in this process, government organizations, universities and research institutions must interact sufficiently in order to develop the potential of interest to ecotourism, ecocultural tourism and scientific tourism. It suggests ways to ensure that tourism is ecologically and socially beneficial.

Key Words: Ecotourism, Reserve, Sustainability, Livelihoods, ecological planning, integration

Introduction

The main focus of most interpretations of sustainable development is the reorientation of understanding society in relation to nature (Redclift 2000). Even though this focus does not necessarily imply such an outcome, most implementation of sustainability has been satisfied with the integration of environmentally sound practices and policies into development programmes and projects (Chifos 2006; Lele 1991). Building on the foundation of increasing environmental awareness, interpretation of economic development as integral to environmental and social systems has gained momentum and has been expressed in a variety of ways, such as redesign of economic processes to work with nature instead of against it (McDonought and Braungart 2002) or rethinking the linkages among livelihood strategies, poverty alleviation and environment (Neefjes 2000; Chambers 1992). Thus, the physical and biological, environmental and economic components of the world system are firmly ingrained in the interpretation and operationalisation of sustainable development.

Protected areas in several countries have been damaged when important ecological aspects of such areas have not been considered. In these areas, plans based on ecological data are needed for land use planning, improvement and development (Jurgen 1993). In most developing countries the purpose of protected areas is to conserve biodiversity and so have failed to recognize the realities of their local socio-cultural and economic environments (Ndenecho 2007). According to Ndenecho (2005) they must protect the cultural, natural and traditional activities of people against the consequences of rapid progress. Effective plans need to conduct all relevant biological, social, physical and economic factors and focus on important resources affecting the ecological integrity of the areas (Gengiz 2006; Sanderson *et al.*, 2002).

Several studies conducted in protected areas have focused on ecotourism or nature tourism as a form of sustainable tourism (Poiani *et al.* 1998; Daniel *et al.* 2005). Recently, research has focused on how protection of local ethnicity can be achieved without impacting on the life of local people by linking social life and environmental protection (Gregory 2005; Barkin 1996). Ecotourism has been suggested as a key to sustainable development of protected areas (Barkin 1996). It provides investment for tourism and enhances the living standards of local people by providing opportunities for employment. Cultural investments, such as historic preservation or dissemination of traditional skills, can also work to provide economic benefits while preserving connectivity with the past (Chifos 2006), that is, it is nurtured and disseminated as poverty is alleviated.

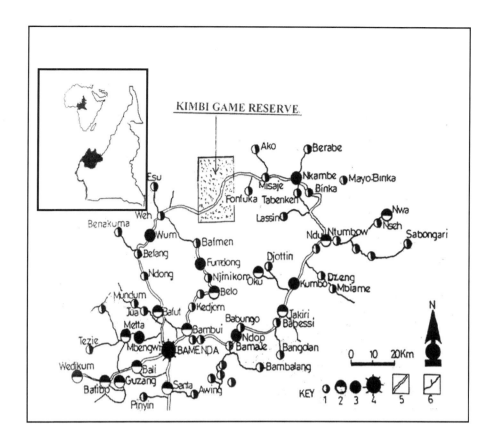

Fig. 1: *Location of the study area with the rural market structure and urban centres: 1. Rural markets; 2. Regional markets; 3. Urban centres; 4. Regional capital; 5. Primary roads; 6. Secondary roads.*

The general trend in ecotourism is to increase experiences by encouraging activities such as long-distance walking, camping, boating, hunting, sight-seeing, swimming, cultural activities, bicycling, observing wildlife and nature, skiing, visiting historical places, and horse riding among others. Generally, instructive activities, for example, wildlife observation, participation in festivals, cultural activities and nature landscapes, attract most attention (Gengiz 2007). In this study, the potential for the sustainable development of ecotourism is assessed in a sample of the Kimbi Game Reserve and the adjacent rural communities. The study was designed to determine the potential use of the area and to suggest ecotourism types likely to be beneficial for local people. It stresses the need for ecological planning and the linking of livelihoods with environmental protection projects.

The grid reference of the study area is Latitudes 6°5'N and 6°40N, and longitudes 10° 19'E and 10° 24'E. The total land surface area covered by the reserve is 6000 hectares (Figure 1). There are 13 villages around the reserve. The altitudinal range is between 950 and 1500m above sea level. Hawkins and Brunt (1995) have described the climate as a "sub-montane cool and misty climate" with an annual mean maximum temperature of 20°C to 22°C and mean minimum of 13°C to 14°C. Annual rainfall varies between 1780 mm and 2290 mm. Most of the rainfall occurs between July and September. A dry season occurs from mid – October to mid- March.

Geographically the area is part of the Cameroonian Highlands ecoregion which encompasses the mountains and highland areas of the border region between Nigeria and Cameroon (Stuart 1986). The area falls within the Afromontane archipelago-like regional centre of endemism that spans the entire African continent. The forests in the area are refugia in montane and sub-montane environments. Conservation efforts have tended to emphasize the protection of biodiversity and so have ignored local livelihoods.

The area is sparsely inhabited by small chiefdoms. In 2005 the population was 1,071 inhabitants with an annual growth rate of 0.85%. By 2015 it is projected to be 1,165 inhabitants. These are subsistence farmers. Poverty is rife in the area as a result of an economy that thrives on subsistence agriculture that yields little income. Unfortunately, the political and economic system which fails to provide local people with land, jobs and food, obliges disenfranchised people to turn to legally protected lands, plants and animals for their needs. Under these circumstances, immediate human survival always takes precedence over long-term environmental goals. However, the government of Cameroon is beginning to realize that ecotourism can be more beneficial to local people in the region over the long-term than traditional extractive activities.

The montane forests are of great ecological significance. They contain several endangered species of plants and animals (Alpert 1993; Ngwabuh 2002). The area is spectacularly beautiful. Several volcanic episodes have created crater lakes, maars and strombolian cones. The reserve is in the Nyos volcanic District, with active gas eruptions and several thermo-mineral springs. The association of fissural and strombolian eruptions produced numerous spatter cones which give outstanding panoramas over the rift basins, forested valleys, and rugged grasslands. The magnificent views, unique wildlife and rich culture all have great tourist potential which could be realized with careful development. Tourists and scientists have shown interest in the wildlife and in the seismic processes of the area.

The game reserve was created in 1963 with the objective of promoting tourism and the improvement of the socio-economic development of the local communities. The reserve status has since remained on paper with little infrastructural investments and promotion of local livelihoods. In recent years it has come under serious threats from geological processes such as lake-basin gas eruptions and anthropic activities.

Methodology

The study focused on the Kimbi Game Reserve and the forest-adjacent villages. Study methods included field observations, data collection and evaluation, using a SWOT analysis. A data base of the reserve was used to derive data on wildlife resources. The Soft Systems Methodology (SSM) which includes Participatory Rural Appraisal (PRA) and Rapid Rural Appriasal (RRA) philosophy was employed to evaluate the current situation. Field observations, informal interviews and secondary data sources yielded data on ecotourism potentials. These were mapped from base maps and updated using field observations and a global positioning system. Base maps and aerial photographs were produced by the National Geographic Institute. The SWOT analysis focused on seven forest adjacent villages (figure 2). The advantages and disadvantages of the reserve were determined with regard to tourism. The analysis was done by determining opportunities and threats and strategic suggestions were presented for ecological planning. In this way a sound understanding of elements, process and practice of local institutions was gained in order to determine appropriate interventions.

Results and Discussions

As the world shrinks, tourists look for new destinations and new experiences. The Highland ecoregion offers both, with fascinating flora and fauna and new climates and terrains. The destinations and experiences in the area include nature landscapes, fascinating wildlife and a rich cultural heritage.

New Landscapes

The area is broken into plateau, fault blocks and steep escarpments. Several recent volcanic episodes have created strombolian cones, crater lakes and maars. The characteristics of the lakes are presented in table 1.

The slopes are littered with landslide scars and some thermo-mineral springs. The physical and chemical properties of these sources may be beneficial for medical purposes, but there are no commercial facilities for using their water. The lakes have not been developed for commercial purposes. This volcanic district which in 1986 was mapped out as a disaster zone and the villagers re-located lies to the south of the game reserve. Its fascinating landscapes and grass savannahs could be carefully developed as part of the reserve (Figure 2).

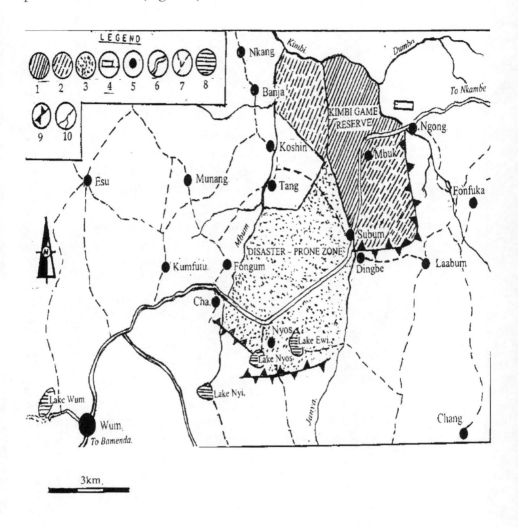

LEGEND: *1: Kimbi Game Reserve, 2: Picturesque zone feasible for the extension of the reserve, 3: Picturesque toxic gas eruption-prone zone feasible for the extension of the reserve, 4: Office and residence of the conservator, 5: Villages, 6: Earth road, 7: Major footpaths, 8: Lakes, 9: Mountain divide, 10: Rivers.*

Fig. 2: *The Kimbi Game Reserve and Feasible zones for the development of ecotourism.*

Wildlife Resources

Wildlife is protected in the Kimbi Game Reserve. It has important potential in terms of flora which has attracted the interest of the International Union for the Conservation of Nature and Natural Resources (ICUN), The World Wildlife Fund (WWF) and the International Council for Bird Preservation (ICBP). It has been identified as one of the most at risk terrestrial ecological regions (Macleod 1986; Stuart 1986; Alpert 1993). A total of 98 plants are recorded in the reserve (Table 2). These belong to 43 plant families (Kwanga 2006). The ecoregion as a whole has one of the highest levels of endemism in the whole of Africa, particularly among birds and vascular plants. For example, 20 bird species are found only in this ecoregion (Stuart 1986).

Table 3 presents the 21 mammals recorded in the reserve. The population drastically reduced since 1973. It was reported that the once abundant species are rarely sited. This is attributed to grazing and farming encroachment, poaching, fire encroachment and poor implementation and management of the reserve status despite the scientific importance of the flora and fauna. A total of 203 bird species are recorded in the reserve (Table 4). These include 45 of the 215 Guino-Congo forest biome bird species and 8 of the 45 bird species restricted to the Sudan-Guinea Savannah. Species of interest include the brown-chested plover *(Venellus supercilious)*. This is an uncommon and local intra-African migrant found to breed in Cameroon and Nigeria (Alpert 1993). Povel's illadopsis *(Illadopsis puveli)* is an uncommon resident in the northern part of the reserve and outlier in savannah flock of 6 birds mostly observed in gallery forests in the Jonja River Valley. The bird life is threatened with habitat loss and fragmentation.

The main attractions are the lakes, the dark green forest of the reserve, gallery forests in valleys, natural pastures on the surrounding plains and hills, and the seasonal colours of plants. These create attractive views. The valleys formed by streams and hills enhance the visual value of the area, and topographic structure is an important feature in creating viewpoints. Present day geomorphic processes and the rich and unique biodiversity are of scientific importance and constitute important destinations for scientific tourism. Unfortunately, these resources are under anthropic pressure.

The forest provides local employment and livelihoods. Timber and non-timber forest products are important local economies with the potential for improvement. The forest and lakes also have strong cultural significance. The main land use effects are forest degradation by the unsustainable harvesting of products, slash-and-burn shifting cultivation, bush fires and range degradation. Agricultural encroachment is a main threat. The proposed improvement of the road from Wum to Nkambe will enhance forest degradation even more by further increasing market access (Figure 2) and hence the agricultural value of the area. Cattle range freely within the periphery of the forest during the rainy season and invade it during the dry season. This prevents regeneration. Serious erosion is now occurring in forest margins aggravated by deliberate burning. The present use of land is having deleterious effects. Hunting is evident at the periphery of the reserve. There are old pit traps, old iron traps and traditional trapping using sticks and twine. Some sling hunting occurs, particularly of squirrels on birds. A programme of reafforestation and regeneration of native species needs to be developed for highly degraded areas in forest borders. Inventories of flora and fauna need to be completed. Population monitoring and ecological studies should be carried out on threatened species.

Table 1: Lakes South of the Kimbi Game Reserve in the Nyos Volcanic District

	Lakes	**Latitude**	**Longitude**	**Altitude (m)**	**Area (hectares)**	**Depth (metres)**
1.	Enepe	6°18` N	10°02` E	697	50	78
2	Wum	6°24` N	10°03` E	1177	45	124
3	Njupi	6°25` N	10°18` E	1020	30	?
4	Nyos	6°26` N	10°18` E	1091	158	208
5	Elum	6°20` N	10°02` E	950	50	35
6	Bénakuma	6°26` N	9°02` E	576	154	132

Cultural Landscape

The villages at the periphery of the reserve and the disaster – prone zone give the area an added attraction of traditional village life, in terms of settlement and variations in land use. The mountain pastures are colonized by semi-normadic tribes who keep cattle, sheep, and horses. Farmers settle in village chiefdoms on plains and valleys (Figure 2). Traditional lifestyle and culture are important and attractive elements for tourists. Traditional architecture is an important element of the cultural landscape, with buildings of wood, bamboo and mud walls and grass-thatched, high, pyramid-like roofs. Numerous carved houseposts support the heavy-thatched roof with its comparatively wide overhang. Door-frames and door-surrounds are carved with several symbolic motifs. Geological processes, configuration of the land, climate and biogeography have shaped the selection of buildings and construction materials. Festivals providing recreation are important in maintaining social cohesion in the chiefdoms. Annual festivals and dances in palace chiefdoms are attractions during the dry season. Tourists experience a variety of traditional meals and rites.

The reserve has no accommodation for visitors, a poor and seasonal road network and poorly developed sites and tourist infrastructure in the nearest town (Wum). These facilities are clearly inadequate for the accommodation needs of tourists. Handicraft production which is already on the decline (Knopfli 1990) can be promoted as an integral part of tourism economy. This is important because the observation of handicraft artisans and the buying of souvenirs or art objects draw tourist interest and spending. The government's reserve policy creates parks and reserves that ignore their human neighbours.

Table 2: Checklist of plant families and the number of plant species in Kimbi Game Reserve

S/N	Family	Number of species
1	*Acanthaceae*	3
2	*Anarcadiacea*	2
3	*Annonaceae*	1
4	*Apocynoceae*	3
5	*Araliaceae*	1
6	*Bignoniaceae*	1
7	*Burseraceae*	1
8	*Combretaceae*	1
9	*Commelinaceae*	1
10	*Compsitae*	2
11	*Costaceae*	1
12	*Cyperaceae*	1
13	*Dracaenaceae*	1
14	*Euphorbiaceae*	6
15	*Graminae*	2
16	*Guttiferae*	1
17	*Lauraceae*	3
18	*Leganiaceae*	14
19	*Malastomocaceae*	1
20	*Meliaceae*	1
21	*Monispermaceae*	2
22	*Moraceae*	2

23	*Musaceae*	1
24	*Myristicaceae*	1
25	*Moraceae*	5
26	*Musaceae*	1
27	*Myristicaceae*	1
28	*Myrtaceae*	1
29	*Ochnaceae*	3
30	*Olaceae*	2
31	*Orchidaceae*	9
32	*Palmae*	2
33	*Piperaceae*	2
34	*Pihosporaceae*	1
35	*Rhamnaceae*	1
36	*Rosaceae*	1
37	*Rubiaceae*	9
38	*Sapindaceae*	1
39	*Ulmaceae*	1
40	*Urticaceae*	1
41	*Verbenaceae*	1
42	*Zingiberaceae*	2
43	*Pendenceae*	1
Total Number of Species		**98**

Source: The conservator, Kimbi Game Reserve.

Table 3: The mammal population recorded in Kimbi Game Reserve

No.	Family	English name	Scientific name
1	Colobidae	Black and white colobus	Colobus guereza
2	Cercopthccidae	Olive baboons	Papio anubis
3	Cercipithecinae	patas monkey	Cercopithecus (Erythrocebus) patas.
4	Cercipithecinae	Green monkey	Cercopithecus (caethiop) tantalus
5	Cercipithecinae	Mona monkey	Cercopithecus (mona) mona
6	Lagosmopha/ baridae	Scrub hare	Lepus scxtilis
7	Rodential/ sciuridae	Striped ground squirrel	Euxerus enythropus
8	Rodential/ sciuridae	Red legged sun squirrel	Heliosciurus rufobrackium
9	Rodential/ sciuridae	African gaint squirrel	Protoxerus stergeri
10	Hytrilidae	crested porcupine	Hystrix cristata
11	Thyronomyidae	marsh canerat	Thryonomys gregorianus
12	Cricetomyinae	Ernin's Giant Rat	Cricetomys Emin's
13	Herspestidae	Slender mongoose	Herpestes sanguinea
14	Viverridae	African civet	Civettictis civetta
15	Procavidae	Rock hyrax	Procavia johustoni
16	Bivini	African Buffalo	Syncerus caffer
17	Tragelaphini	Bushbuck	Tragelaphus scriptus
18	Cephalophini	Bay duiker	Cephalophus dorsalis
19	Cephelophini	Blue duiker	Cephalophus monticola
20	Reduncini	Rob	Kobus kob
21	Reduncini	Water Buck	Kobus ellipsiprymus defassa

Source: The conservator, Kimbi Game Reserve.

SWOT Analysis

The Kimbi Game Reserve within the Nyos Volcanic District is rich in natural and cultural treasures. The strengths (S), weaknesses (W), opportunities (O) and threats (T) of ecotourism resources were identified:

- **Strengths and Advantages**
  - The area is rich in wildlife (plants and animals) and natural landscapes of touristic and scientific importance.

167

–   It possesses rich cultural values, handicraft production, traditional houses, settlements, festivals, rites and food.

–   Local people are welcoming and have a positive attitude to tourism.

–   Annual festivals and dances are organized in chiefdoms (palaces).

–   Life is traditional and tranquil in a typical African setting.

–   The area has an ecological potential to increase the destinations and experiences for worldwide tourism.

- **Weaknesses or disadvantages**

-   The area is far from the provincial capital city (Bamenda) and other urban centres.

-   There are clearly no tourist infrastructure and service facilities.

-   The reserve is grossly under-staffed with no staff educated for tourism.

-   The area is enclaved in difficult topography and remote from urban centres. There will be high investment costs.

-   Tourism in the region has no advertisement and marketing activities and agencies.

-   Local people and tourists are insensitive to environmental issues.

-   No master management and development plans to take advantage of the opportunities offered by ecotourism.

-   Lack of tourism marketing and promotion agencies.

- **Opportunities**

-   Integrating rural livelihoods in conservation projects for local employment and poverty alleviation.

-   Promoting, sustaining and reviving a disappearing cultural heritage.

-   Protecting and sustaining the rich biodiversity.

-   Promoting the participation of local people in biodiversity protection.

-   Promoting tourism and biodiversity conservation by linking culture, the environment and livelihoods.

- **Threats**

-   Total absence of infrastructure and waste disposal systems.

-   Increasing human pressure on fauna, flora and natural landscapes.

- Erosion of the cultural values through production and commercialization to suit the taste of tourists and through the adoption of foreign values.
- Poorly structured and unplanned village settlements and houses that can be developed as cultural villages.
- Underdeveloped environmental consciousness and threat of pollution.
- Risks from catastrophic landslides and gas eruptions from crater lakes.

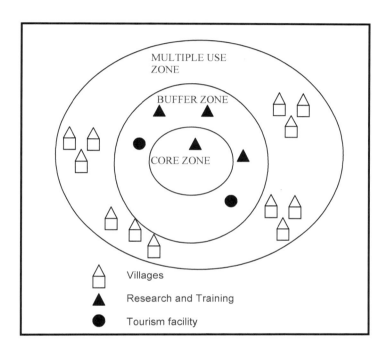

Figure 3: *A model for the integration of ecotourism, rural livelihood and biodiversity protection in traditional societies.*

Most local people in the area benefit very little from tourism. An innovative project for the development of ecotourism must alleviate impacts of tourists and maximize the income generating potential of ecotourism. The Kimbi area is the home of people who continue to use resources in a traditional way. This designs an encouraging model for poor communities.

Permanent villages are situated in the multipurpose use area around the reserve. The Kimbi area has a rural population of 1,071 inhabitants according to 2005 statistics. These are people who use resources in traditional ways. The area should be divided into different zones, for example, intensive farming land in the multipurpose-use area, seasonal grazing areas in foothills, special management zones along tourist routes in the core and buffer zones, protected areas with high biological richness in the core zone, protected areas with high cultural richness in the multi-use area (villages) and wilderness area in the high peaks. The degassing and monitoring of Lake Nyos can constitute an important element of research and scientific tourism.

There can be no meaningful conservation without the active involvement of local people. Fees paid by visitors should go directly in financing a variety of conservation, education and development projects in the area. Local entrepreneurs can be trained in lodge management, hygiene and marketing. Forest guards can be hired; latrines built, trails repaired, schools and clinics built for local people and provide local tree nurseries for reforestation projects by local people. Recreation throughout the year should be planned, while protecting natural habitats, wildlife and local cultural heritage.

The following are some suggestions to ensure that ecotourism is ecologically and socially beneficial:

- Information on local culture and on sensibilities: Prepare and disseminate information on the history, geography, ecology and culture of the area. This should prevent the violation of local culture and sensibilities.
- Environmental impact: Develop defined trails and camp sites.
- Resource Impact: Minimize the use of scarce resources such as fuel, food and water.
- Cultural impact: Sensitize visitors to respect the privacy and dignity of local people and to be considerate of religious and cultural sites and practices. They should be aware of cultural pollution as well as environmental pollution.
- Wildlife impact: Sensitize visitors not to harass wildlife or disturb plant life, and not to buy animal products such as animal skins, shells and feathers from endangered species.
- Environmental impact: Encourage tourists to contribute to protecting the local environment, that is, to combine ecotourism with work on clean campaigns, delivery of educational materials to local schools or to nature clubs.
- Advocacy and education: Visitors should be encouraged to be involved in letter-writing, lobbying, or educational campaigns to help protect the landscapes, culture and biodiversity.

Table 4: Checklist of birds in Kimbi Game Reserve

Non-Passerines		Passerines	
Family	No. of species	Family	No. of species
Ardeidae	1	*Campephagidae*	2
Anatidae	1	*Crvidae*	1
Accipttridae	14	*Dicruridae*	1
Apodidae	3	*Eurylaidae*	1
Alcedinidae	8	*Emberizidae*	1
Charadrudae	1	*Estrildae*	10
Columbidae	4	*Fringillidae*	1
Cuculidae	8	*Hirundinidae*	7
Coludae	1	*Landidae*	2
Capitonidae	8	*Motacillidae*	4
Caprimulgidae	1	*Monarchidae*	2
Bucerotidae	1	*Muscicapioae*	3
Falconidae	1	*Malaconotidae*	10
Indicatoridae	1	*Nectarinidae*	11
Jacanidae	1	*Oriolidae*	2
Musophagidae	2	*Pycronotidae*	10
Meropidae	4	*Platysteiridae*	3
Osittacidae	2	*Paridae*	1
Phasianidae	2	*Passeridae*	1
Picidae	3	*Ploceidae*	6
Rallidae	3	*Syviidae*	24
Scopidae	1	*Sturnidae*	7
Strigdae	1	*Thurdidae*	6
Threskiornithidae	1	*Timalinidae*	2
Upupidae	1	*Zosteropidae*	1
TOTAL	74	**TOTAL**	129
GRAND TOTAL = 203 species of birds			

Source: Summarized from the archival materials of the Kimbi Game Reserve

Conclusion

Tropical countries like Cameroon, beleaguered as they are, have established parks and reserves as a way of saving biodiversity. Take a chunk of forest, the reasoning goes, make it a park or reserve, and charge tourists to visit. But parks that ignore their human neighbours and parks that are poorly protected are doomed to fail. Careful planning and investments are required to overcome the weaknesses and threats. In planning most attention should focus on the needs of local people, that is, integrating their culture, livelihoods and environmental awareness in tourism development. In this process local people, government organizations, universities, research institutions and society as a whole must interact sufficiently in order to develop components of interest to ecotourism, ecocultural tourism and scientific tourism. The study posits that the struggle to save species and unique ecosystems cannot be divorced from the boarder struggle to achieve a new world order in which the basic needs of all are met. The development of ecotourism in partnership with local communities and conservation projects can restore local livelihoods. In this way villages can learn how to manage the wildlife and landscapes in a sustainable manner, making sound livelihood decisions without sacrificing their cultural values. Environmental impact and social impact assessments and mitigation strategies are necessary.

References

Alpert P 1993. Conserving biodiversity in Cameroon. *Ambio* 22: 33 – 107

Barkin D 1996. Ecotourism A tool for sustainable development. http.//www.planeta.com/planeta /96/0596 (Retrieved, December 14, 1996)

Chambers R 1992. Sustainable livelihoods: The poor's reconciliation of environment and development. In: Ekins P and M. Max-Neff (Eds.) *Real-life economics: Understanding wealth creation.* London: Routledge

Chifos C 2006. Culture – environment and livelihood; potential for crafting sustainable communities in Chiang Mai. *Int. J. Environment and Sustainable Development,* 3:315-332.

Daniel L, Manning R, Krymkowski D 2005. Relationship between visitor-based standards of quality and existing conditions in parks and outdoor recreation. *Leisure Science,* 27: 157-173.

Gengiz T. 2007. Tourism, an ecological approach in protected areas: Keragol-Sahara National Park, Turkey. *Int. J. of Sustainable Development and World Ecology,* 14:260-267

Gregory T 2005. Conflict between global and local land use values in Larvia's Gauja National Park. *Landscape Research*, 30:415-430

Hawkins P, Brunt M 1965. *Soils and ecology of West Cameroon*. Rome: FAO Report

Jurgens CR 1993. Strategic planning for sustainable rural development. *Landscape and Urban Planning*, 27:253-258

Knopfli H 1990. *Crafts and technologies: Some traditional craftsmen of the Western Grassfields of Cameroon. Part 2: Woodcarvers and blacksmiths*. Basel: Basel Mission Printing Press.

Kwanga MJ 2006. *Wildlife management: Case Study of Kimbi Game Reserve*. BSc. Long Essay (Unpublished), Yaounde: University of Yaounde.

Leenhartdt O, Menard J, R Temdjim 1990. *Rapport sur l'inventaire des lacs maar au Cameroun*. Yaounde : Mission Francaise de Coopération.

Lele S 1991. Sustainable development: a critical review. *World Development*, 19:607-621

McDonought W, Braungart M 2002. *Cradle to cradle: Remaking the way we make things*. New York: North Point Press.

Macleod H 1986. *The conservation of Oku Mountain forest*. Cambridge: ICBP Project Report.

Ndenecho E N 2005. Conserving biodiversity in Africa: Wildlife management in Cameroon. *Loyola Journal of Social Sciences*, 2:209-228

Ndenecho E.N 2007. Population dynamics, rural livelihoods and forest protection projects in sub-Saharan Africa: experiences from Santa, Cameroon, *Int. J. of Sustainable Development and World Ecology*, 14:250-259

Neefjes K. 2000. *Environment and livelihoods: strategies for sustainability*. London: Oxfam Publishing.

Ngwabuh B. A 2002. *Annual report of the Kimbi Game Reserve*. Bamenda: NW Delegation for Environment and Forest.

Poiani K, Baumgartner J, Buttnick S, Gren S, Hopkins E, Ivy G, Seaton K, Sutter R 1998. A scale-independent site conservation planning framework in nature conservation. *Landscape and Urban Planning*,43:143-156

Redchift M 2000. Sustainability: life chances and livelihoods. London: Routledge.

Sanderson E, Redford K, Veddez A 2002. A conceptual model for conservation planning based on landscape species requirements. *Landscape and Urban Planning*, 8:41-56.

Stuart S.N. 1986. *Conservation of Cameroon Mountain forest*. Cambridge: ICBP Project Report.

Chapter 10

Climate Change, Livelihoods and Protected Area Management

Case Study: Cameroon Protected Areas

Summary

There is a growing recognition that natural ecosystems, both large and small, could provide a suite of ecosystem services related to climate change, ranging from protection against immediate physical impacts (rising temperatures, unstable climates, rising sea level) to providing additional insurance against the predicted instability of agriculture, fisheries and water resources. The chapter describes the general ecological and biodiversity features, distribution per biogeographic region of both the biodiversity and protected areas, and appraises the management. It further examines the significance of particular impacts and how protected areas might relief symptoms. The main issues examined include: disaster mitigation covering floods, droughts, landslides, and coastal erosion; fires, biodiversity; water security; the need for rapid crop adaptation; and food security, including the potential of crop and fish stock failure. Finally, some recommendations are made on how protected area management can contribute to the wider efforts at mitigating climate change impacts, and incidentally increase support and resources for management.

Key Words: ecological benefits, economic benefits, protected areas, climate change impacts, managing to relief impacts.

Introduction

Available literature points to the fact that well-designed and managed protected areas may ameliorate some of the problems caused by climate change, with benefits well beyond the boundaries of the protected areas. These potential benefits are predicted from a number of assumptions about the way in which natural ecosystems will respond to changing climate. This chapter seeks to describe the general ecological features and biodiversity potentials, the distribution of protected areas per biogeographic region, appraises the management and outlines some of the known and expected benefits that protected areas offer to resilience against climate change. It identifies the scope for maximizing these benefits.

175

Ecological and Biodiversity Potentials

The diversity of relief and latitudinal extent of Cameroon has produced several micro-ecological climates that are reflected by a rich and varied biodiversity. One can encounter several ecological niches over very short distances in the mountain and sub-montane areas. Figure 1 presents the various vegetation zones, and the zone of ancient and recent destruction and disappearance of the rainforest. The overlay of climate change impacts and human impacts has contributed to the savannization of this zone. This also is evidence of the southward shift in vegetation types, that is, the recession of forest types to the advantage of invasive weedy species, graminae, fire-tolerant and more xerophytic species. Savanna of post forest is spreading their antennae into the once humid forested areas. The transition is from humid forest to tree and shrub savanna, shrub savanna, shrub steppe and grassland savanna. These derivatives, however, reflect the intensity of the human impact on the environment, edaphic factors, altitude, latitude and aspect. Future climate change will exacerbate both the anthropogenic or human-related impacts and the climate-related impacts. This will endanger several ecosystem goods and services. These are important potentials to be protected and sustainably managed. Table 1 and 2 present some wildlife data for the country.

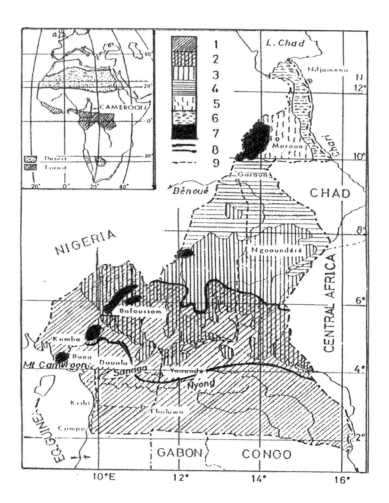

Figure 1: *Vegetation zones (after Letouzey, 1979; Loung, 1973) of Cameroon and main survey routes. 1: Dense moist forest, 2: Savanna of post forest, 3: Shrub savanna and grass savanna, 4: Tree savanna and savanna wood land, 5: Tree and shrub steppe, 6: Seasonally flooded tree and shrub steppe, 7: Mountain and subalpine formations, 8: Zone of ancient and recent destruction of dense moist forest, 9: Main survey routes.*

Photo: *Thorn bush savanna: Chad Plain*

Photo: *Dry Sudan savanna biogeographic zone*

Photo: *Sahel savanna biogeographic zone: Diamare*

Photo: *Wooded savanna biogeographic zone: Benue*

Photo: *High savanna in the Bamileke plateau*

Photo: *Montane forest on Mount Cameroon*

Photo: *Dense rainforest*

Photo: *Exploitation of the rainforest*

The country possesses 297 species of mammals, 848 species of birds. 300 species of amphibians, 9000 species of plants (Gartland, 1992), 29 species of primates and 39 swallowtail butterflies (USAID. 1991'). Some 156 species of plants are endemic (Gartland, 1992). Much of Cameroon's potential wealth thus lies in its natural resource base. This resource base includes forest, biodiversity, and soil and water resources. This biodiversity provides great potential for eco- tourism, for timber and non-timber forest products. The forests are also of great scientific value for the world community.

If we consider only the vertebrates: Cameroon has 2 1% of the fish species found on the African continent, 48% of mammal species. 50% of batrachian species, 54% of bird species and 30 to 75% of reptiles. The presence of these animals is closely linked to the vegetation in which they live. There are many ecosystems in Cameroon. We can distinguish three main Zoographic zones: the forest, Savannah and Sahel zones.

Mammals are because of their size the most spectacular element of the wildlife population and contribute enormously to the tourist resource base of the country. There are five families of primates. These are all forest species except for three species of monkeys and one type of bush baby. 34 species of carnivores are present. Although the lion and the jackal are still well represented in the national parks, the panther, cheetah, lynx, bush cat, golden cat, hyena and light-coloured fox have all become very rare. Elephants, which used to very numerous, survive the sparsely populated areas, but it is common to meet the Savannah elephant in the national parks. The rhinoceros has seen its numbers diminish drastically in recent years. The hippopotamus, originally found in all Cameroon rivers, has disappeared from many of them. Buffalos and antelopes are still well represented. The country also possesses the three suidae of Ethiopia; Warthog, river hog and the giant forest hog. The order of rodents comprises many species. Bats are numerous.

Stemming from the diversity of ecosystems, the bird population is extraordinarily rich with, to date, 942 species having been identified. Numerous sea birds are seen at the coast in the dry season (grills, petrels, skuas, puffins). The coastal lagoons and mangrove swamps harbour cormorants, sterns, herons, egrets, sandpipers, godwits, curlews, and plovers. The forest region houses the largest and richest bird population. Tauracos, parrots, guinea fowl, black partridge, pigeon, shrike and magpie are very rare. Taurocos have been classified as endangered due to habitat loss. In the Savannah eco-climate are large birds (jabine, black Abyssinian horntail, marabou, crowned crane, ibis, stork, heron, bateleur eagle, hoopoe, vulture, kite). The greatest gatherings of birds here can he seen around water sources during the dry season. The Sahel has considerable populations of ostriches, bustard, guinea fowl, black partridge, stone curlew, lapwig, nightjar turtledoves and sparrows. Some are sedentary while others are migratory. The ubiquitous species include: the magnificent black and white bald buzzard, cattle egret, pygmy kingfisher, jacana, cormorant, pagoda cock and omnipresent magpie.

The country is rich in reptiles. The crocodile, turtle and tortoise population is well known. The snake, lizard and chameleon population have not been well studied and identified. Three of the crocodiles existing in Africa are present: Nile crocodile, long-nosed crocodile and snib- nosed crocodile. Among the tortoises and turtles are 5 types of sea turtles, 10 types of freshwater turtles and 4 types of tortoise. More than 150 species of snakes are found in the whole country. 15 of them are considered dangerous to man. With about 300 species of amphibians, Cameroon is the richest country in amphibians. The amphibians are composed of those of the lowland forest, secondary formations, mountains and savannah ecological niches. The most remarkable life forms in the forest are the goliath frog and hairy frog. The goliath frog is 30cm long and weighs 2.4kg and is the largest in the world. Most of these are endangered by habitat loss.

Man's aggressiveness towards nature is a well-known phenomenon all over the world. Cameroon is no exception. The population explosion is the main cause of the drop in the wildlife population. The actions of man on the environment, and thus on the wildlife, are harmful. This is particularly remarkable in the rain forest, where agriculture and lumbering have greatly modified the environmental structure and ecosystem functions.

Table 1: Comparison of number of species of main flora and fauna represented in Africa and Cameroon

	Group or class	Cameroon	Africa	% Cameroon / Africa
Flora	Phanerogames	8.000	45 to 50.000	16 to 17%
	Cryptogams			
	Pteridophytes	264	500 to 600	44 to 52%
Fauna	**Fish (1)**	530	2510	21%
	Batracians (2)	200	400	50%
	Crocodiles	3	4	50%
	Tortoise	12	40	30%
	Reptiles (3) Lizards	160 – 170	300 – 400	40 to 56%
	Snakes	160 – 170	250 – 300	53 to 68%
	Birds(4)	942	1.738	54
	Mammals(5)	126	263	48%

Source: Encyclopaedia of the United Republic of Cameroon, Vol. 1(1979) Les Editions Africaines

Table 2: Comparison of mammals represented in the world, Africa and Cameroon

Order	Family	Sub-family	World	Africa	Cameroon
Insectivore:	Erinaceidae		14	6	1
	Potamogalide		3	3	1
Lagomorphe	Leporidae		59	7	1
Rodents	Sciurisae		285	25	11
	Anomaluridae		9	9	7
	Thryonomyidae		6	2	2
	Hystricidae		20	4	2
	Pedetidae		2	1	0
Pholidotes	Manidae		7	4	3
Primates	Lorisidae		5	2	2
	Galagidae		5	4	
	Cercopithecidae		49	28	16
	Colobidae		24	7	3
	Pongidae		3	2	2
Carnivore	Canidae		35	11	4
	Mustelidae		42	7	5

	Viverridae		70	29	16
	Hyaenidae		4	4	2
	Felidae		37	10	10
Tubulident	Orycteropidae		1	1	1
Sirenian	Trichechidae		3	2	1
Hyracoide	Procaviidae		9	3	2
Proboscidian	Elphanitidae		2	1	1
Perissodactyle	Equidae		12	4	0
	Rhinocerotidae		5	2	1
Artiodactyle	Hippopotamidae		2	2	1
	Suidae		8	4	3
	Tragulidae		2	1	1
	Giraffidae		2	2	1
	Bovidae	*Hippotraginae*	6	6	1
		Ruduncinae	10	10	4
		Alcelaphinae	9	9	2
		Antilopinae	20	13	1
		Caphalophinae	14	14	9
		Neotraginae	7	7	3
		Madoquinae	4	4	0
		Caprinae	28	2	0
		Bovinae	16	1	1

Source: Encyclopaedia of the United Republic of Cameroon, Vol. 1(1979) Les Nouvelles Editions Africaines

Man has always altered habitats, but today, the demographic boom of the country, introduction of the cash crop economy, the needs of subsistence farming, commercial and subsistence hunting and organization of the human or cultural space place inordinate strain on habitats essential to many species (see Tables 3, 4 and 5). Alteration of habitat is the most significant single factor in extinctions. Habitat is destroyed by human civilizations spreading into fields, forests, oceans, mountains, riparian areas and water ways, roads, strip mining, dams, housing projects, airports, farms and cities usurp wildlife habitat. Industrial activities especially along the coast have altered several ecological niches.

Table 3: *Crocodiles found in Cameroon and their habitats*

Scientific name	Maximum length	Habitat
Crocodylus niloticus	6 matres	Ubiquitous
Crocodylus cataphractus	4 metres	Coastal zone
Ostrol / Emus tetraspis	2 metres	Rainforest

Source: Cameroon Encyclopaedia, Vol. 1, 1977, ENA

Table 4: Principal land tortoises of Cameroon and their habitats

Family	Scientific name	Maximum length	Habitat
Testudinidae	*Geochelone sulcata*	80cm	Sahel
	Kinixys belliane	20cm	Savanna
	Kinixys erosa	30cm	Forest
	Kinixys homeana	20cm	Forest
Pelomedusidae	*Pelomedusa subrufa*	25cm	Savannah
	Pelusios gabonensis	30cm	Forest
	Pelusios castaneus	35cm	Savannah
	Pelusios niger	30cm	Savannah / Forest
	Pelusios carinatus	25cm	Forest
	Pelusios adansonii	20cm	Sahel
Trionychidae	*Trionyx triunguis*	80cm	Savannah/Forest
	Cyclanorbis senegalensis	50cm	Savannah
	Cyclanobis elegans	50cm	Savannah
	Cyclanobis aubryi	50cm	Forest

Source: Cameroon Encyclopaedia Vol. 1, 1979, ENA

Table 5: Main species of snakes and their habitat

Family	Scientific name	Maximum length	Habitat
Elapidae	*Naja nigriocollis*	2.20 m	Ubiquitos
	Naja melanoleuca	3.10 m	Forest / Savannah
	Naja haje	2.50 m	Savannah / Sahel
	Naje katiensis	2.000 m	Savannah / Sahel
	Boulangerina annulata	3.00 m	Forest
	Pseudohaje goldi	2.60 m	Forest
	Dendroapis jamesoni	2.80 m	Forest
	Dendroapis polylepis	4.00 m	Forest
Viperidae	*Causu lichtensteini*	0.60 m	Forest
	Causus resimus	0.75 m	Forest / Savannah
	Caussus maculates	0.50 m	Savannah
	Bitis arietans	1.60 m	Forest / Savannah
	Bitis gabonensis	2.20 m	Sahel / Savannah
	Bitis nasicornis	1.20 m	Forest
	Echis carinatus	0.80 m	Savannah
	Cerastes cerastes	0.80 m	Sahel

Source: Cameroon Encyclopaedia Vol. 1, 1979, ENA

However, the main factor in the disappearance of the wildlife remains hunting in all its forms. The pressure exerted by hunting has considerably increased through the growing numbers and sophistication of firearms. Added to hunting, which often takes place in defiance of all regulations, are trapping activities and the use of pesticides. The current tendency is towards a drop in numbers of all synergistically interesting animal species and even to the rareness of certain species to such an extent that there is the danger of them disappearing altogether. Most of them are today only found in national parks, reserves and protected areas which themselves are poorly managed.

The elephant populations have declined drastically during the past decades. The killing of elephants by poachers to supply the ivory markets primarily of Japan, the United States and Europe is the main cause. Elephants are also jeopardized by loss of habitat as agriculture reaches deeper into the wilderness. The elephant's complex social structure has been greatly damaged and in some areas it is not clear whether surviving elephants will be able to sustain their populations through reproduction. Other species may become affected because the elephant is a keystone species, one that shapes its environment. The changes that the elephant brings to its environment are beneficial to a variety of other Savanna species. Loss of the elephant could have a drastic impact on the tourist business, it may also affect the rapidity with which trees populate savannas emptied of elephants; potentially changing the types of species that can use the land.

Biogeographic Distribution of Protected Areas

The distribution of protected areas per biogeographic zone and the surface area of each protected zone are presented in Table 6. There are five main wildlife reserves covering a land surface area of 575,000 hectares. These reserves are protected by government regulations and equipped with amenities for tourists. These include Waza, Benue, Bouba-Ndjida, Kalamaloue and Mozog-Gokoro reserves. These reserves are found in the Sudanian -Sahelian eco-floristic zone:

- Waza wildlife reserve was created in 1968. It has a land surface area of 170.000hectares. This is the best known and the most spectacular wildlife reserve in the country. The main animals found here include the lion, cheetah, elephant, hippotragus, waterbuck, hartebeest, cob, giraffe, wartlog and the panther. There are several birds such as the ostrich, heron, goose, pelican, egret and the vulture among others. Lodging camps for tourists are perched on the Southern slopes of the hills overlooking Waza town.
- Benue wildlife reserve has a land area of 180.000 hectares along the Ngaoundere-Garoua highway. Traversed by the Benue River, there are several hippopotami and crocodiles in the shallow riverbed. Other important animals include buffalos, derby elands, antelopes, lions and elephants. The reserve has two lodging camps.
- Bouda-Ndjida wildlife reserve is located in the Cameroon-Chad frontier between latitudes 8° and 9°N. It occupies an area of 220.000 hectares and is the habitat for rhinoceros, giant eland, antelopes, lions and buffaloes.
- Kalamaloue reserve covers an area of 4,500 hectares near the border town of Kousseri. Like the Bouba-Ndjida and the Mozogo-Gokora reserve there are no lodging camps.
- Mozogo-Gokoro wildlife reserve is found near Koza pass. It has an area of 1400 hectares and is poorly developed in tourist facilities.

Apart from these reserves in the Savannah ecological climate, there are eight forest reserves that are rich in biodiversity. While the wildlife reserves are well developed in tourist amenities and routes the forest reserves do not have such facilities and therefore are not developed to receive tourists (Figure 2, 3 and 4)

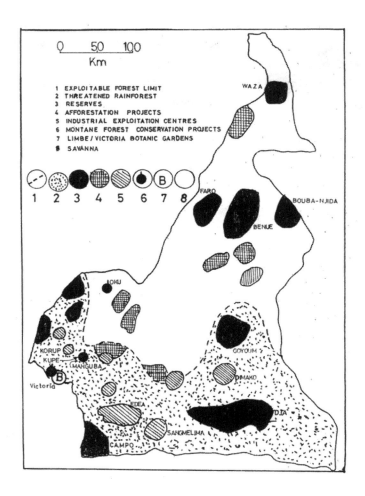

Figure 2: *Forest conservation projects in Cameroon*

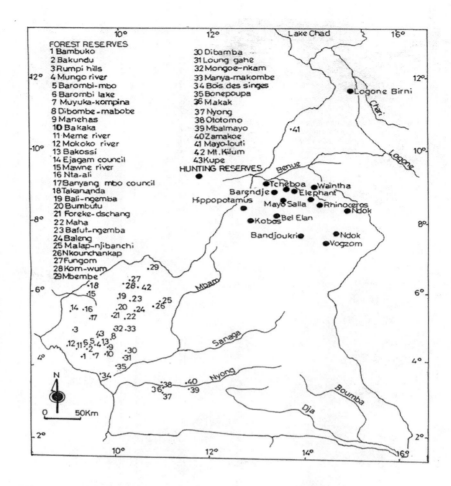

Figure 3: *Hunting and forest reserves of Cameroon situation as in 1992*

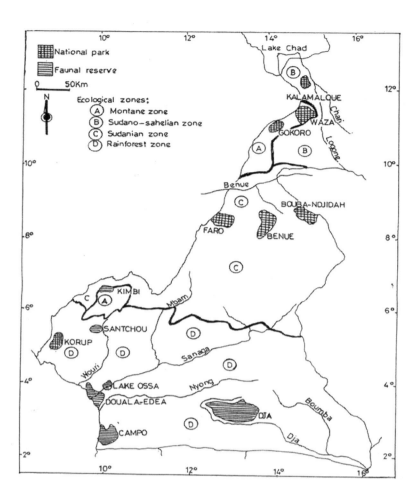

Figure 4: *National Parks and faunal reserves of Cameroon*

Table 6: Distribution of forest reserves per biogeographic region

Forest Reserve	Area (hectares)	Biogeographic zone
Kalfou reserve	4000	Sahel eco-climate
Faro reserve	335,000	Sudan eco-climate
Pangar and Djerem	300,000	Sudan eco-climate
Kimbi reserve	5,000	Montane eco-climate
Dja reserve	520,000	Rainforest eco-climate
Douala – Edea reserve	160,000	Rainforest eco-climate
Campo reserve	300,000	Rainforest eco-climate
Lake Ossa reserve	4,000	Rainforest eco-climate

Within the rainforest region Korup is the only forest national park out of the seven national parks. The other six are located in the Sudano-Sahelian region (Faro, Benue, Bouba-Njida, Mozogo-Gokoro, Waza and Kalamaloue). Korup National Park contains Africa's oldest rainforest and is over 60 million years old with a high level of endemism. There are 1000 species of plants and 1300 animal species including 119 mammals and 15 primates. Of the total listed species, 60 occur nowhere else and 170 are listed as endangered. It was established in 1937 and would have largely disappeared by 2025 but for conservation work initiated by the World wide Fund (WWF) for Nature. The conservation programme centres on a management area of 126,000 hectares plus a surrounding buffer zone of 300.000 hectares (Pearce, 1994).

In the Mount Cameroon region there are areas protected to maintain nationally significant landscape characteristics of the harmonious interaction of resident people and land while providing opportunities for public enjoyment through, recreation and tourism within the normal life-style and economic activity of these areas. (Table 7)

Photo: *Poaching is a major cause of the extinction of animal species. Villagers with a dead elephant after a fruitful hunt in a forest reserve in the South Cameroon rainforest. (after A. S. Neba, 1987)*

Table 7: Protected areas of the Mount Cameroon Region

No.	Protected Area	Area (Ha)	Year Established
1	Korup National Park	211.675	1937
2	Ejagham Forest Reserve	74.850	1934
3	Takamanda Forest Reserve	67.599	1934
4	Mative River Reserve	53.872	1951
5	Rumpi Hills Forest Reserve	45.843	1941
6	Bayang-Mbo Forest Reserve	42.606	1936
7	Nta-Ali Forest Reserve	32.982	1935
8	Bambuko Forest Reserve	26.677	1950
9	Southern Bakundu Forest Reserve	19.425	1940
10	Mokoko River Forest Reserve	9.065	1952
11	Bakossi Forest Reserve	5.517	1956
12	Meme River Forest Reserve	5.180	1951
13	Mungo River Forest Reserve	4.662	?
14	Barombi-Mbo Forest Reserve	855	1950
15	Botanic Garden Limbe	375	1892
16	Buea Fuel Plantation	300	1953

The Limbe Botanic Garden is bilaterally funded by the government of Cameroon and the United Kingdom. It is focused on tourism, environmental education, scientific research and conservation. There is also a herbarium with accommodation for visiting scientists. The Limbe zoological Garden is an annex of the Botanic Garden. Over the years the animal population in the Zoo has been declining due to the lack of proper management. There is an on-going project in the Zoo that seeks to create a primate sanctuary centre for indigenous endangered species. These two gardens are part of a wider project known as Mount Cameroon Project. The project seeks to assess areas of high biodiversity in the Mount Cameroon region and to prepare them for gazattement as forest reserves. The identified areas include: Etinde Mountain forest, Onge forest and Moliwe-mabeta forest. Mount Kupe Forest Reserve and Takamanda Gorilla Sanctuary are essentially game reserves with the objective of identifying and conserving endangered species and endemic species. Mount Kupe reserve covers 2000 hectares of land.

The montane forests of Cameroon to the west of the country are unique. They have one of the highest levels of endemism in the whole of Africa, particularly among birds and vascular plants. Mount Oku was identified the only extensive area of montane forest left in the Bamenda highlands. This protection reserve was established in the 1930s. By 1984 it needed critical conservation action. This was rendered by the International Council for Bird preservation (ICBP). The remaining forest covers 7000 hectares. Mount Oku Forest Reserve is characterized by a large number of endemic species. Altogether 53 species of montane forest birds are found in the Western highlands, 20 of these are true endemics. The Preuss's monkey *(Cercopithecus preussi)* is one of the most important mammals to occur. It is classified by the International Union for conservation of Nature and Natural Resource (IUCN) as endangered. It has only been recorded in a few patches of forest in Cameroon and Eastern Nigeria. Several small mammals have subspecies endemic to the Oku Forest. A few species of frogs *(Xenopus sp.)* are endemic to the forest. This protected area has good scientific and tourist potentials but lacks tourist amenities.

Protected Area Management

There is general shortage of personnel in the national parks and wildlife reserves. For Instance Dja Wildlife Reserve, which measures some 526,000 hectares, has only one conservator and three guards. In addition, nearly all protected areas do not have adequate operational means of transportation, let alone good communication. The guards are equipped with obsolete weapons and are short of ammunition whereas poachers have more efficient weapons (Besong and Ngwasiri, 1995). These problems certainly greatly constrain biodiversity and eco-tourism industry.

While it is apparent that biodiversity protection has gathered 'considerable momentum in the country in recent years, there is still a wide gulf between rhetoric and policy objectives, on the one hand and the reality of policy and project implementation on the other. Numerous environmental laws and regulations enacted in 1994 remain unenforced, programmes or projects poorly implemented, while measures coined to protect or rehabilitate ecosystems often impinge negatively on livelihoods at the village or local level or involve benefits which accrue mainly to local elites. The experience reveals the following problems:

- Insufficient attention to socioeconomic and cultural situation of local people whose livelihoods depend on resources found in parks and preserves;
- Attempts by development agencies or the state to protect or rehabilitate ecosystems in one particular area are often contradicted by other development measures which degrade the environment.

- Many laws and regulations governing land use in parks and preserves remain unenforced

- It has been usual of protected area status to be imposed on a specific area without prior consultation with the local population. This results in social conflict in and around these areas which are generally associated with four factors: the ways parks and preserves have been established; the process of land acquisition; the invasion and occupation of land in protected areas; and resource use in such areas by the local population.

- The piecemeal and partial character or non-implementation of many conservation policies and programmes, as well as the difficulties of sustaining positive initiatives through time, and replicating successful interventions. This is largely as a result of dependence on external aid and expertise.

- Lack of adequate consultation and clarification concerning the demarcation of preserves and parks as well as the limited capacity of conservation agencies to enforce the protected area status.

- It is not uncommon to find that certain local interests such as logging companies or lumber merchants have the necessary financial and administrative resources, as well as the connections with local administrative authorities, to obtain the documentation required by the forestry Law for timber exploitation.

It is now being realized by development agencies that the "conservationist" approach to biodiversity conservation has failed to come to grips with crucial social issues. In most protected sites technocratic formulas have often been imposed which generally ignore the socioeconomic and cultural situation of thousands of families whose livelihoods depend on the forest. This approach has provoked social conflicts which often undermine the possibility of implementing and achieving basic conservation objectives. Under such circumstances, non-enforcement of regulations becomes an explicit strategy of the state to reduce conflicts. Coupled with limited human and financial resources necessary for the administration of parks and protected areas, most reserve status exist only on paper.

Most important, the sustainable management of wildlife requires understanding that future threats will be driven simultaneously by global phenomena such as the greenhouse induced climate change, as well as local and regional resource management schemes. Climate change will fundamentally change ecosystems composition and functioning.

Managing Protected Areas to Relief Climate Change Impacts

Carefully designed and managed protected areas can help relief problems beyond the park boundary. In some cases protected areas are simultaneously a potential buffer against a particular climate-related problem and at risk from the same problem, creating a tension and the need for some tough decisions from protected area managers. This requires a lot of research and monitoring in order to learn about many of these impacts. Opportunities to use protected areas as buffers against climate change require two additional management approaches (WWF, 2003):

- *Planning to maximize the benefits of protected areas in relieving the symptoms of climate change:* The importance of assessing protected area management effectiveness must be recognized and climate change elements must be added to these assessments. This apart from enhancing the effective management of the protected area will also aid in planning future protected areas. Such assessments can be carried out at ecosystem or landscape level. Management actions can then be put into a national or regional context.

- *Using protected areas to help mitigate the effects of climate change:* Available literature shows that protected area managers are already using land and water resources to buffer against climate change without recognizing the connection. However, more systematic research is required to quantify beneficial impacts and to refine management interventions to maximize these benefits. Efficient management of protected areas can achieve the following:

- *Flood:* The presence of natural vegetation generally reduces storm-related erosion and landslides. Deforestation in several areas has led to flooding (Calder, 2000; Kaimowitz, 2002).

- *Drought:* Maintaining natural vegetation can provide an important insurance policy in areas prone to drought. Drought effects have been exacerbated by prior forest loss (WWF, 2003)

- *Coastal impacts:* Protected areas can play a role in disaster mitigation in marine and coastal areas. Sea level rise and increased storm damage puts coastal communities and small islands at particular risk. The disappearance Cape Cameroon before our eyes is clear evidence. Building physical barriers against the rising sea is technically difficult and colossally expensive for a poor country. This stimulates a new approach to integrated management based on the mangrove ecosystem. A review of marine ecosystem services suggests that the mangrove forests are the most cost effective option. Unfortunately, the consequences of their destruction are already evident in Limbe, Douala and Cape Cameroon. The restoration of the mangroves is extremely important (Moberg and Ronnback, 2003; Field, 1999).

Unfortunately, this ecosystem is paradoxically seriously threatened by climate change. Protected area managers will be faced with a series of hard decisions, balance the benefits from mangrove ecosystem, the chances of its surviving climate change and the cost and benefits of protection trade-offs may be necessary.

- *Fire:* Climate change will add an additional element to the already complex relationship between fires and natural systems. Hotter, drier conditions tend to increase fire frequency resulting in changes in vegetation as more fire-tolerant species become common. Forest fires can directly affect protected areas as is often the case in the Kilum and Ejim Forest Reserves. (Macleod, 1986; Goldammer and Seibert, 1992). Training in community fire management is therefore an important part of management (Karki, 2002).

- *Biodiversity:* Protected areas aim at protecting biodiversity. But managers must simultaneously also design management strategies that will increase the resistance and resilience of the biodiversity to climate change.

- *Water security:* Protected areas can be managed to guarantee the quantity of water supply. Forests increase or stabilize water supply. Some forests may also increase net water flow from watersheds. Good quality water, free from sediments is also guaranteed. This provides an argument for the protection of montane cloud forest and upland watersheds in river basin systems.

- *Genetic stress:* changing climate will increase stress on both new and traditional crop varieties. There is need for crop breeding programmes to respond to this change. Climate change will cause a decrease in crop varieties (McCarthy *et al.*, 2001). Wild relatives of modern crops therefore have an important role to play in kick-starting the breeding of new strains under time pressure. Protected areas can be designed to protect sources of crop genetic material.

- *Food security:* Climate change will also disrupt agricultural systems and fisheries. Protected landscapes and seascapes provide a potential buffer in three ways (McCarthy *et al.*, 2001): by providing breeding grounds for commercial species, by providing wild foods to the poorest members of society in time of crop failure and preserving genetic resources needed for adaptive breeding.

Conclusion

From the above review, the management of protected areas should therefore focus on:

- *Maintaining and increasing large reserved areas:* Large unfragmented reserves are likely to be most useful in both resisting climate change and providing resilience within a landscape, that is, increasing core reserve areas, linking reserves and developing effective buffers are crucial first steps.

- *Plan protected areas with disaster mitigation in mind:* Protected areas can protect human communities from climate-related floods, landslides and droughts.

- *Recognize the role of protected areas in maintaining terrestrial food and water supplies:* Small changes in management can allow the natural vegetation in protected areas to help supply emergency food and forage, increase or stabilize water yields which are all likely to be in shorter supply in the future.

- *Site marine protected areas to maintain fisheries:* As fish stocks suffer from multiple stresses of over-exploitation, pollution and climate change, ways of maintaining breeding stocks become more important. Portions of the Cameroon's Atlantic Ocean need to be protected.

- Ensure that the above measure do not impinge negatively on livelihoods at village level. This can be achieved by participatory planning and management involving all stakeholders.

References

Asong, A. (2001) Forest degradation and forest reserve strategies in the South West Province. In: Dunlop, J, and Roy, W. (eds.) *Culture and Environment*. University of Strachdye/University of Buea.

Besong, J. and Ngwasiri, C. (1995) The 1994 forestry law and rational forest resource management in Cameroon. PVO – NGO/NRMS Cameroon Publication, Yaounde.

Biwas A. K (1992) Environment and sustainable development for Cameroon. Report of a multidisciplinary and multi-institutional mission on the environment, Yaounde.

Calder, I. R. (2000) Land use impacts on water resources. *Background Paper No.1. Electronic Workshop on Land-Water linkages in Rural Watersheds.* FAO, Rome.

CAMPER/USAID (1993) USAID Cameroon programme for environmental reform. CAMPER.

Field, C. D. (1999) Rehabilitation of mangrove ecosystem: an overview, *Marine Pollution Bulletin, Vol. 37*, p. 8-12.

Gartland, S. (1992) Cameroon. In. Sayer, J. (ed.) conservation atlas of tropical forests, Africa. Harcourt and M. Collins, London.

Goldammer, J.G. and Seibert, B. (1992) the impact of drought and forest fires on tropical lowland forest of East Kalimantan. In: J.G. Goldammer (ed.). *Five in the tropical biota-ecosystem processes and global challenges.* Springer-verlag, Berlin.

IUCN(1978) Threatened mammals of Africa. The IUCN Red Data Book. International Union of Nature and Natural Resources, Cambridge.

IUCN (1985) 1985 United Nations List of National Parks and Protected Areas. IUCN, Gland.

Kainmowitz, D. (2002) Useful myths and intractable truths: the politics of the link between forest and water in Central America. Center for International Forestry Research, Bogar, Indonesia.

Karki, S. (2002) Community involvement in and management of forest fires in southeast Asia. Project Fire-Fight SE Asia. WWF, ICUN and European Union, Bogor, Indonesia.

Letouzey, (R. (1979) Vegetation. In: J.F. Loung (ed). *Atlas of the United Republic of Cameroon.* Jeune Afrique, Paris, p. 20-24.

Loung, J. F. (1973) Le Cameroun. Collection A. Journaux, Hatier, Paris. 96p.

Macleod, H. (1986) Conservation of Oku Mountain forest, Cameroon. *ICBP study Report No. 15.* Cambridge.

McCarthy, J.; Canziani, O.; Leary, N.; Dokken, D.; and K.S. White (eds.). Climate change 2001: Impacts, adaptation, and vulnerability. IPCC, Cambridge University Press.

MCP (1998) Report on the elaboration of pluralistic sustainable structure for the management and conservation of natural resources in the Mount Cameroon Region. MCP, Buea.

Moberg, F. and Ronnback, p. (2003) Ecosystem services of the tropical seascape: interactions, substitutions and restorations. *Ocean and Coastal Management, Vol. 46*, p. 27-46.

National Geographic society (1990) The emerald realm: Earth's precious rain forest. NGS, Special Publication Division, USA.

Neba. S. (1982) Modern Geography of the Republic of Cameroon. Neba Publisher, Cameroon.

Ngome, M. (1992) Environmental education in Cameroon: Problems and Prospects. WWF, Cameroon, Yaounde.

ONADEF (1993) Cameroon's forests: for a sustainable and lasting management. National Forestry Development Agency, Yaounde.

Pearce, D. W. (1994) Valuing the environment: Past Practice, future prospects. In: Ismail, S. and Steer, A. (eds.) *Valuing the environment. Environmentally Sustainable Development Proceedings Series No.2* World Bank. Washington, D.C.

WWF (2003) A user's manual for building resistance and resilience to climate change in natural systems. World Wildlife Fund, New York, 240 p.

202

Chapter 11

Sustainable Forest Management by Communities

Summary

Mainstream initiatives to protect and rehabilitate forests in developing countries have failed to integrate the physical and ecological with social, economic and political processes. In view of the paucity of data on the linkages between the ecological and social processes at grassroots level, there is a need to collect original data through field research. Understanding the relationship between farming, forest management and dependent livelihoods is one of the important aspects of community forestry. Participatory mapping is a simple method that provides an effective and efficient tool for field workers to collect the socio-economic and bio-physical data they need to understand the relationships between people, forests, culture, religion, livelihoods and their farming systems. Such data is necessary for planning and implementation of community forestry programmes. This concluding section of the book describes the methodology of participatory mapping and provides guidelines for the application of Participatory Rural Appraisal (PRA) tools and a checklist of data collection activities for community forest management projects.

Key Words: Community forestry, forest user group, participatory mapping, Participatory Rural Appraisal, sustainable management.

Introduction

Many communities, especially in rural areas of developing countries, are directly dependent on natural ecosystems for their livelihoods. Biodiversity (the total variety of life on earth) incorporates all those species (animals and plants) which form the basis of people's livelihood (foods, medicines, fibres, fuelwood, timber, harvestable products such as honey, mushrooms, vegetables and many others). In addition to these economic and sustenance values, forests have cultural value to local people and provide important ecosystem functions (water protection for example). Sustainable management of natural systems reduces the risk of people becoming impoverished and can provide a "safety net" during times of hardship, especially for the very poorest. It represents an opportunity to increase people's economic well-being, while re-asserting their sense of identity, dignity and community.

203

Communities adjacent to forests are aware of their values and important resources derived from them, but these communities and the responsible government departments lack the capacity to achieve effective forest conservation and management. In particular, the skills needed for appropriate, community-based, participatory approaches to natural resource management are lacking. There is no widespread public constituency to support forest conservation and natural resource management. There is an urgent need to design and implement projects which will enable local people sustainably manage their natural resources for the benefit of the local communities while maintaining the ecological value of forests in the long-term. This objective can be achieved through working with local communities to develop appropriate, community-based institutions and systems for the management of forests. Management plans are developed using participatory methods. These are designed to meet the needs of communities while also maintaining forest biodiversity and ecosystem functions. In this way, degradation of forest will be halted and, rehabilitation of degraded areas promoted. Activities of such projects include investigation of patterns of forest use, institution building, development and agreement of management plans, forest demarcation, habitat improvement work and monitoring of forest resource condition and use.

The primary partners in such projects are the forest-adjacent communities, with the Ministry of Forest and Environment (MINEF) as the official project partner and supervisory body. There will therefore be a need for capacity building for conservation and sustainable forest resource management within communities, traditional authorities, local NGOs through participation in forest management planning, and implementation, through joint meetings and exchange visits and through provision of specific training and support. A broad local constituency in support of the conservation of the natural heritage can thus be built through an awareness and information campaign linked to all other project activities and using appropriate media, field visits, presentations and information material. Direct beneficiaries of such projects include:

- Those people dependent on the use of forest resources to provide for their livelihoods (usually the poorest and the marginalized).
- Those people farming land adjacent to forests. Specific development projects can be initiated to reduce pressure for forest clearance, for example, through sustainable farming practices and the development of alternative forms of income-generation.

- Those in communities who place important cultural, religious or other social value on the forest and their species.
- Technicians and forest officers in government who can gain through training and experience in sustainable forest management and participatory approaches to resource use and development.
- Local NGOs who can be strengthened institutionally and to develop skills and capacity which can help ensure their long-term organizational sustainability and effectiveness.
- Women, who are associated with harvesting of particular products. They will gain in forest management through the development of participatory, equitable forest-management institutions and targeted development projects.

The sustainable forest management by communities will also derive indirect benefits. Such benefits will accrue to:
- All those involved with marketing and processing of forest products.
- Those people downstream of water catchments protected by forests.
- Children, and future generations, for whom sustainable management of natural resources today means that they are available tomorrow, so that options are maintained.
- Humanity as a whole concerned for the future of the earth's biodiversity.

In order to enhance natural resource management in forest-adjacent communities, the government of Cameroon has opted for community forestry. Human and institutional capacity in the design and implementation of such a programme and projects suffers from incoherencies. The following section develops guidelines for effective and efficient collection of data necessary for such programmes. It emphasizes the participation of local people and their empowerment.

Community Forestry

Community forestry is defined as the situation where the responsibility for managing state-owned forests rests with the local villagers. The purpose of such hand-over is to give villagers the right to use these forests for both semi-subsistence agriculture and market needs. Field workers involved in helping villagers develop strategies for the sustainable use of community forests need to understand the relationships between farms, rural people, markets and forests. This requires information on (Kackson *et al.*, 1994):
- Land tenure,

- Land use,
- Cropping patterns,
- Livestock husbandry practice,
- Location and condition of local forests,
- Traditional or historical patterns of forest use,
- Existing use rights of common forests
- The type, seasonal use and importance of inputs from forest to farm,
- The perceptions of forests users, and
- The conflicts and cooperation within forest user groups and between user groups and others.

Community forestry involves entrusting the management of local forests to a "user group". A user group is a group of people with mutually recognized rights to whom the benefits derived from the management accrue. In Cameroon as in many developing countries, very little information is available to field workers unless they collect it themselves. Maps and records are rare and when available are often incorrect or incomplete. Collecting information from the field is complicated by the fact that field workers cannot afford to spend extensive periods of time collecting data. They often have heavy workloads and have to cover large geographic areas. Fortunately, community forestry does not require the collection of very technical data or the preparation of highly accurate maps. In community forestry one of the more important needs is field workers that can promote dialogue with and between villagers in a non-threatening manner. From such dialogue the field worker can obtain relevant information while simultaneously helping villagers to identify, and find solutions to, their problems and needs.

Participatory rural appraisal (PRA) and, to a lesser extent, Rapid Rural Appraisal (RRA) methodologies are well suited to gathering the information needed for implementing community forestry and for promoting dialogue between field workers and villagers (see, for example, Anonymous, 1989; Bartlett and Nurse, 1991; Chambers, 1992; Mascarenhas, 1992; Lightfoot *et al.*, 1989). Both PRA and RRA methodologies use techniques such as informal discussions, transects, village and community profiles, time lines and sketch mapping. The value of this technique is that they allow the field worker to involve villagers as participants in the process of problem identification and problem resolution. Such a process is more likely to address the real needs of local or rural communities and find solutions that are effective, efficient and sustainable.

The Use Of Pra For Community Forestry

Bartlett and Nurse (1991) and Nurse, Bartlett and Singh (1992) describe a simple PRA Methodology used to support forest user groups. Field workers record information on a set of simple format and a sketch map. The formats are intended to guide field workers in discussion with villagers during informal surveys and the maps provide a simple and convenient format for recording and displaying the results of the survey. The sketch maps for this purpose provide a good indication of the ground-truth, as well as helping community forestry field workers to better understand the local use of the forest in question.

Sketch maps provide a particularly convenient way of recording and illustrating information about forests and the local communities that use that forest. Sketch maps can be used:

- to define the boundaries of common forests,
- to locate physical features such as watercourses, ridge lines and trails, and
- to record the type and condition of a forest.

Such information provides a basis for identifying potential areas of community forests, defining forest user groups, providing technical advice, discussing management options with forest user groups, setting planning objectives and monitoring progress. If a more formal map is required, the information on a sketch map can be transferred to a topographic map using the features common to both maps to tie in various points on the map.

Shortcomings with the PRA methodologies used in community forestry are that field workers tend to use the formats inflexibility by treating them as a structured questionnaire and they develop a sketch map without adequate consultation with local villagers. The effect of this is that the methodology becomes more "rapid" than "participatory", often resulting in poor quality information being recorded and sketch maps that contain neither accurate nor useful information. The main reasons for this are lack of skills and lack of consultation with local forest users. Participatory mapping allows field workers to acquire a more reliable understanding of forest use practices and local requirements of forest products.

Participatory Mapping

Establishing Rapport

The first steps of participatory mapping process are to develop a basic understanding of the geography of the area to be mapped and to establish rapport with local villagers. This involves walking around and getting to know the geographical setting, and talking to local people about what interests them. This is called establishing rapport (Fisher, Malla and Jackson, 1994).

Section of site

Once rapport has been established a suitable site is selected to prepare the map. The ideal site is a level ground that has a reasonably unobstructed view of the area of interest and is clear of vegetation.

Invitation of key informants

A group of key informants from the area is invited to participate in the exercise. Key informants should have adequate knowledge about the issues and area of interest and preferably include both male and female informants as each group often has a different understanding of forest use patterns and use rights. The process begins when the field worker after giving the reasons for drawing a map then scratches a line onto the ground to represent a prominent feature of the landscape, for example, a stream, ridge, path or road. The name of this feature is elicited from the key informants and written on a piece of paper. The paper is placed on the ground beside the mark representing the feature and held in place by a stone.

Participatory development of the map

The map is developed by informants scratching marks on the ground, or using coloured powders to represent features such as streams, ridges, villages, roads and forest boundaries. As each feature is drawn on the ground its name is added to the map. Sometimes there is a disagreement between the informants as to where a particular feature is to be located. When this occurs the field worker should not intervene too early or they will risk breaking the participatory nature of the exercise if the villagers perceive that field worker is trying to dominate.

At the end of the first stage the map scratched on the ground shows the location and names of ridges, rivers, streams, villages, roads and important boundaries. This provides the basic framework on which the rest of the map is constructed. In the second stage, areas of common property forest are mapped on the location map by placing handfuls of grass, leaves and weeds on the ground to represent the location of each forest patch. After this, the following information can be added to the basic map:

- location of administrative boundaries,
- location and names of facilities (schools, church, water sources),
- the number of households and type of people in each village or hamlet,
- type and location of farmlands,
- location and name of forests used by local people,
- use patterns of local forests (type and products), and
- the flow of products from the forest to farm.

Information such as names of features and numbers of households are written onto slips of paper and placed on the ground wherever the villagers say the features should be located on the map. Once the map on the ground is completed the field worker sketches the map onto a sketch pad or graph paper. Care is taken to ensure that the general layout of the area and the names of features is correct. It is important that the field worker promises to deliver a copy of the map once it is complete.

To ensure accuracy and to avoid conflicts it is best if the mapping exercise is repeated at several other sites in the locality using different informants. During each exercise the paper copy of the participatory sketch map is adjusted by adding new information and discarding information that is considered inaccurate. It is important to recognize that key informants may only be able to supply accurate information for the area in their immediate vicinity. Because of this, field workers should take care to only build a map that covers an area that can be seen from the mapping site.

The sequence of building a participatory map is important. The best method is to initially ask questions that are not threatening to villagers, for example, names of villagers and location of administrative boundaries and forests. Once the villagers begin to understand the process and feel less threatened, the field worker can then attempt to elicit more sensitive information such as use patterns of local forests.

If needed a larger scale participatory map can be developed for a single forest or part of a forest. To do this the key informants need to be people who have relevant knowledge about the history and present use of particular forest in question. The aim of developing large scale maps is to enable the field worker and villagers to better understand issues such as forest use patterns, forest condition, and the potential of the area to provide for the needs of forest users.

In locations where there are large areas of forests, local forest users often refer to the forest as consisting of smaller contiguous forests with internal boundaries defined according to availability of forest products and accessibility. Locating and recording such boundaries is essential to community forestry as they often represent the division of the forest into areas that have discrete user groups and the field worker may need to negotiate the handover of individual patches of forest with a number of separate user groups, as opposed to handing over a single forest to a large user group.

Participatory mapping provides more reliable and cost effective way to collect, store and display information than methods and formats that were previously used. They are very useful for obtaining and recording bio-physical and socio-economic information needed for implementing community forestry. These maps can be produced at various scales. Smaller scale maps can form the basis for a preliminary PRA exercise, complementing other PRA tools such as informal interviews, focus group sessions, transect and time lines. Larger scale maps allow more detailed investigation of an individual user group and their community forest. These maps are appropriate for use in planning and implementing community forestry.

Application of the Pra Tools by Field Workers

1. Informal Interviewing
- Field workers are made (more) aware of the;
* importance of checklists and interview guides;
* need to be sensitive to key informants;
* utility of visualization methods to enhance dialogue;
* importance of listening and learning from local people;
* need to ask open-ended questions;
* need to probe responses carefully;
* need to verify information through triangulation;
* importance of recording responses and observations fully and when it is best to record;
*potential use and importance of information from informal interviews for preparing village and forest profiles;
* different types of informal interviews (e.g. group or individual) and

scenarios (e.g. in village meetings, in peoples' houses, in peoples' fields, at water sources, in shops or bars, and offices) that are possible;
* different types of behaviour and what constitutes good and bad interview practice;
* things that can go wrong during an interview and what can be done to cope; and,
* potential for sabotaging a saboteur or saboteurs.

- Encourage field workers to have (in private) some personal reflections on their own behaviour in the office and field.

- Encourage group reflection on behaviour in all informal interviews.

2. Calendar (Time charts)

- Field workers are made (more) aware of the range of diagrams and their applications.

- Field workers understand the use of different diagrams:
* in analyzing differences;
* in identifying trends and changes over time;
* for discovering connections and correlations;
* with literate and illiterate people;
* to attract and focus attention;
* for representing complex objects or processes; and,
* for assisting in decision making / problem analysis.

3. Wealth Ranking

- Field workers are made (more) aware of:
* what wealth ranking is;
* the need for wealth ranking;
* the potential use and importance for identifying the households that have the greatest impact and dependence upon the forests;
* the power of this tool but also that it must be used well (e.g. must use different, independent informants and must triangulate with mapping and direct observation)
* possible biases (e.g. informants want themselves and their friends classified as poor in order to get more benefits: wealthy people may not understand poverty and not be able to distinguish between different degrees of poverty (i.e. "they are all poor"); informants may not know households very well).

4. Ranking / Scoring

- Field workers are made (more) aware of:

* ranking and criteria concepts;
* purposes of ranking;
* different ranking methods;
* purposes of weighing;
* how to use pair wise ranking; and,
* potential for personal and/or professional biases in ranking exercises.

5. Time-lines
- Field workers are made (more) aware of how time-lines can show qualitative change over different periods of time.
- Field workers made (more) aware of the potential use and importance for preparing village and forest profiles.
- Field workers understand that there are many different ways of visualizing changes over time, including dated lists, diagrams, and maps.

6. Venn Diagram
- Field workers are made (more) aware of how Venn diagrams can show institutional relationships in general and institutional relationships outside and inside a village.
- Field workers are made (more) aware of how Venn diagrams are a very useful aid to thinking about and understanding complex relationships and identifying strong groups (and elites) within a village.
- Field workers understand the processes involved in preparing a Venn diagram to capture information about existing groups and organizations and to elicit suggestions as to how relationships between groups could be improved.
- Field workers are able to highlight contrasting perceptions of the same institution(s).

7. Debriefing and Process Analysis
- Field workers to be made (more) aware of the importance of sequencing to facilitate triangulation, the influence of their individual/ group biases, and the importance of achieving good reporting and analysis.
- The Survey Team Leader to be (more) aware of need to take a high profile position throughout the analysis and round-up sessions, the importance of encouraging relaxed and informal discussions, and the use of visual, revolving, innovative report back methods.

Checklist of Topics for Pra Data Collection Activities

The following sections provide preliminary lists of topics, issues and areas of knowledge that should be explored during data gathering activities using different PRA tools. Some example questions are provided to illustrate what sort of information should be sought. However, it is important to note that these example questions should not be used as a questionnaire and that other questions be posed by field workers to explore issues in depth. In no way should data gathering be limited to the issues and example questions provided in the following checklists. The outputs from complementary research activities and experience gained by field staff should be used to modify and further refine the checklists provided here.

After having built rapport and established positive relationships with local people, field workers should explore the following topics using participatory mapping, time charts, direct observation, informal interviews and forest walks with key informants, interest group meetings, small group meetings, and informal interviews with individual forest users and user group members (where such groups exist).

- Past or current arrangements made by local people to protect or regulate access to a particular tree, plant species, product or forest area for which there is no single owner.
- Past or current systems for distributing forest products or resolving disputes over access to forests or forest products which are common property.
- The presence of local techniques or knowledge for planting, protecting, tending and manipulating vegetation to establish or regenerate trees and forests for which there is no single owner.
- The presence of local techniques or knowledge for selecting individuals, species, or areas of forest for either harvest or retention to achieve a future yield or forest structure.
- The past or current existence of groups of people with mutually acknowledged rights of use and access to either specific forest products, trees, forests or sites within the forest. These use-rights are mutually acknowledged if claims to use specific forest products or sites in particular area are regarded as legitimate by other people in the same area (the group that hold use-rights as legitimate by other people in the same area (the group that hold use-rights over the same product, forest or site are referred to as a user-group)

- The residential location of forest users, whether they are members of a user-group or not.
- The past or current existence of locally recognized roles or organizations which either implement regulatory rules or make decisions over the protection or use of either specific forest products, trees, species, forests or sites within the forests. It should be recognized that the existence of roles or organizations is not a necessary element of indigenous forest management systems, but merely indicates a level of formality that has developed. A system can exist without a formal structure, consisting of a simple set of locally agreed rules and practices for regulating the way people use forests.
- How indigenous systems of forest management actually worked in the past and, or are working currently.
- The strengths and weaknesses of past or existing systems of indigenous forest management according to issues such as equity in distributing benefits, capacity for resolving conflicts, sustainability of production, efficiency of utilization, and potential for achieving the forest management objectives of local people and the nation.
- The existence of key informants and locally recognized opinion leaders who may either have knowledge about current forests or forest uses, influence the way local people use forests, or display initiative and new strategies for managing individual trees, species or forests.
- The existence of groups of people who have, or are likely to have similar sets of interests in regard to how forest products, species, forests, and special sites within forests are managed (referred to here as forest-related interest groups).
- For each forest-related interest group, user-group or type of forest user, consider the following questions:

* What products are obtained, when and from where?

* What are the local perceptions about ownership over the resources in question?

* are there any shortages or other problems in obtaining these products?

* Who is entitled to use the products from specific areas?

* What are the local names of different areas or paths where forest products are collected?

* How does the present condition of the forest, or the current availability of products, compare with the situation of say five, ten or 20 years ago? If there have been changes, what are the reasons given by local people for the changes?

* do people get a fair share and if not, why?

* are there any problems or disputes in obtaining products and how are they normally resolved?

* are there any systems or practices which provide protection to specific sites, trees, species or forest areas?

* How is the knowledge about these practices disseminated and maintained in rural communities?

* do these systems work well, and if not why not?

* What are the preferences for different species and product types?

* Who collects each product, when and why (e.g. are there gender, age or wealth differences)?

* What products flow to which settlements and households, from each forest area under investigation, and when are they collected?

Calendar (time charts)
- Calendars or time charts can be used to elicit information about:
* The timing and relative quantities of forest product collection
* Employment for men/women (young & old)
* Sources of income and their relative importance
* Household expenditures
* Seasonal cash flows
* Women's economy in each group
* Men's economy in each group
* Stresses on land use system
* Cropping patterns / mixtures
* Risk reducing strategies

Mapping Checklist

Social Mapping
- Social maps can be used to elicit information about:
* Location, name and numbers of people in each household
* Location of households not represented at meetings
* Land tenure situation
* Types of households (wealth ranking)
* Social structures
* Ethnic groups
* Locations of employment
* Infrastructure (e.g. trails, schools, roads, canals)

- Physical maps can be used to elicit information about:

* The location of (all) entry points to forest
* History and rate of land-use changes
* Perceptions of environmental stress
* Local tree technical knowledge
* Local crop technical knowledge
* Location of (all) water sources
* Present land uses
* Farming systems
* Stresses on land use system
* Presence of planted trees
* Reasons for planted trees
* Residential location of different forest-users

Direct Observation

Wealth Ranking
- Type of roof, walls and floor
- Standard of house maintenance (when last painted / repaired)
- Land holding size and type
- Main productive activity

This section to be developed through the complementary research activities.

Use of Forest Products
- Species and quantities in storage (e.g. woodpiles)
- Species being harvested
- Species not being harvested

Time Lines
- Time-lines can be used to elicit information about:

* Changes in employment for men and women (young/old)
* Sources of income
* History of forest use and tenure
* History of rate of forest use changes and reasons
* Park encroachments
* Land use history

Venn Diagrams
- Venn diagrams can be used to elicit information about:

* Existing groups and organizations
* Village decision makers / elites

216

* Social structures
* Ethnic groups

Ranking / Scoring
- Ranking systems can be used to elicit information about:
* The varying importance of income sources
* Expenditures most difficult to meet
* Local tree/crop technical knowledge
* Local tree/crop preferences
* Most important problems
* Preferred solutions
* Preferred criteria for selecting participants in Project interventions.

Acknowledgements

The author acknowledges the use of material from Network Paper 17e: Participatory mapping for rural community Forestry. The Rural Development Forestry Network is funded by the European Commission and Overseas Development Institute, U.K.

References

Anonymous (1989) An Introduction to Participatory Rural Appraisal for Rural Resources Management. Program for International Development, Clark University, Worcester, Massachusetts and National Environment Secretariat Ministry of Environment and Natural Resources, Nairobi, Kenya.

Bartlett, A. G. and Nurse, M. C., (1991), 'A participatory approach to community forestry appraisals', *Banko Janakari* 3 (92: 25 – 38).

Carson, B. (1985), 'Aerial Photography as a Base for Village Level Planning inNepal', Land Resource Mapping Project, Kenting Earth Sciences Limited, Kathmandu.

Carson, B. (1988), 'HMG/USAID F/FRED Training Workshop on Local Level Forest Land Use Planning', Winrock.

Chambers, R. (1992), 'Participatory rural appraisals; past, present and future', *Forests, Trees and People Newsletter (15/16): 4.*

Fisher, R.J. Malla, Y. B. and Jackson, W. J. (1994), 'Forestry Work in Villages: A Guide for Field Workers' (Second Edition), Nepal Australia Community Forestry Project Technical Note 1/94, Kathmandu.

Fox, J. (1986), *Aerial Photographs and Thematic Maps for Social Forestry*, Social Forestry Network Paper 2c, ODI, London.

Fox, J. (1988), 'Diagnostic Tools for Social Forestry', East-West Environment and Policy Institute, East-West Center.

Jackson, B., Nurse, M., Singh, H. (1994), "Participatory mapping for community forestry". Rural Development Forestry Network Paper 17e, ODI, London.

Lightfoot, C. Axinn, N. Singh, P. Botrall, A. and Conway, G. (1989), *Training Resource Book for Agro-Ecosystem Mapping*, International Rice Research Institute, Philippines and Ford Foundation, India.

Mascarenhas, J. (1992), 'Participatory rural appraisal and participatory learning methods: recent experiences from MYRADA and South India', *Forests, Trees and People Newsletter (15/16)*.

Nurse, M. C., Bartlett, A. G. and Singh, H. B. (1992), 'Rapid Appraisal of Forest Resources in Community Forestry', Nepal Australia Community Forestry Project.

Nurse, M.C., Singh, H. B., Paudyal, B.R. and Bonjan, S. (1993), 'Beat Level Planning: Towards the Development of a Management Information System for Community Forestry' Discussion Paper, Nepal Australia Community Forestry Project.